CIVIL
SOCIETY

CIVIL SOCIETY

The American Model and Third World Development

HOWARD J. WIARDA

UNIVERSITY OF MASSACHUSETTS

Westview
PRESS

A MEMBER OF THE PERSEUS BOOKS GROUP

Copyright © 2003 by Westview Press, A Member of the Perseus Books Group

Westview Press books are available at special discounts for bulk purchases in the United States by corporations, institutions, and other organizations. For more information, please contact the Special Markets Department at the Perseus Books Group, 11 Cambridge Center, Cambridge MA 02142, or call (617) 252-5298. ·

Published in 2003 in the United States of America by Westview Press, 5500 Central Avenue, Boulder, Colorado 80301–2877, and in the United Kingdom by Westview Press, 12 Hid's Copse Road, Cumnor Hill, Oxford OX2 9JJ

Find us on the World Wide Web at www.westviewpress.com

A Cataloging-in-Publication data record for this book is available from the Library of Congress.
ISBN 0-8133-4076-4 (HC) ISBN 0-8133-4077-2 (Pbk.)
The paper used in this publication meets the requirements of the American National Standard for Permanence of Paper for Printed Library Materials Z39.48–1984.

10   9   8   7   6   5   4   3   2   1—05   04   03

CONTENTS

TABLES

PREFACE

This book is the result of two converging interests. The first is a lifelong interest in the comparative politics and development of the Third World: Africa, Asia, Latin America, and the Middle East. The second is a lifelong interest in American foreign policy, particularly as it applies or misapplies in the Third World, an interest that only intensified after moving to Washington exactly twenty years ago and not only writing about but also becoming closely involved as a participant in the policy process. The main question I have been wrestling with all these years is whether these two—Third World development and American foreign policy—can ever meet, achieve understanding and compatibility, let alone go forward in tandem. The record is not auspicious.

When I first came to Washington on a more-or-less permanent basis in 1981, I published a small monograph entitled "Ethnocentrism and Foreign Policy: Can We Understand the Third World?"[1] The answer I arrived at, a resounding No, was exceedingly controversial at the time and got me in considerable trouble with the powers-that-be at my then-employer, The American Enterprise Institute for Public Policy Research (AEI), which presumed to know what was best for the Third World. A couple of years later, when the Reagan administration launched Project Democracy, the forerunner of today's National Endowment for Democracy (NED), I wrote an equally controversial essay, which was then republished in numerous anthologies and foreign-language editions, entitled "Can

Democracy Be Exported?"; again the answer was on the negative side.[2]

More recently at the Center for Strategic and International Studies (CSIS), I have published another provocative monograph entitled "Cracks in the Consensus: Debating the Democracy Agenda in U.S. Foreign Policy,"[3] which has also been controversial among colleagues, policy makers, and fellow scholars.

The present monograph builds on this earlier work even while venturing into the new terrain of civil society, the latest panacea in U.S. democracy assistance. It asks the question, "Is Civil Society Exportable?" in much the same way that my earlier essay inquired if democracy was exportable. If posed in this way, of course the answer has to be negative; but here as in the earlier work the issue is more complex than that. The real questions are: Can the United States, whose political institutions were so powerfully shaped by the Lockean, Madisonian, Tocquevillian conception of democracy, interest group pluralism, and civil society, ever understand Third World societies cast in Confucian, Islamic, and non-Western conceptions that are very different from our own? And what happens when American foreign policy, the American foreign aid program, and American nongovernmental organizations (NGOs), all strongly influenced by this same American liberal tradition, encounter and run up against societies and nations whose values, understandings, and priorities are based on distinct cultural, social, and political institutions and understandings different from our own?

The book is organized as follows: Chapter 1 introduces the main themes and questions. In Part II we deal with the theory and concepts: Chapter 2 traces the history of civil society in Western political thought and examines its diverse meanings, while Chapter 3 deals with the predominant response in Third World countries to social modernization: corporatism. In Part III we report successively on a series of case studies carried out by the author in Sub-Saharan Africa, East Asia, Latin America, and the Middle East. The Conclusion spells out the implications of the study for U.S. foreign policy.

This study has been generously supported and funded by a number of institutions and foundations. My home university, the University of Massachusetts, provided me with a sabbatical leave year; my department, Political Science, has been generous with its leave policy. The Earhart Foundation and the Fulbright program supported my research in Central and Eastern Europe on the related themes of post-communist democratization and integration; the Austrian Institute for International Affairs (OIIP) in Vienna and the Central European University (CEU) in Budapest served as my genial hosts during that period. The staff, colleagues, and leadership of the Center for Strategic and International Studies (CSIS) and the Woodrow Wilson International Center for Scholars have been supportive of my work and generous with their comments on it. Finally and most importantly, the Aspen Institute's Nonprofit Sector Research Fund generously supported my travel and research in Africa, East Asia, Latin America, and the Middle East. As always, Dr. Iêda Siqueira Wiarda provided critical familial, logistical, intellectual, and moral support.

None of these agencies or persons is responsible for the views expressed; that responsibility, for good or ill, rests with the author alone.

Howard J. Wiarda
Washington, D.C.
August 2002

NOTES

1. (Washington, D.C.: American Enterprise Institute for Public Policy Research, 1985).

2. Published initially as Occasional Paper No. 157, Woodrow Wilson International Center for Scholars, Washington, D.C., 1984; and in Kevin J. Middlebrook and Carlos Rico (eds.), *The United States and Latin America* (Pittsburgh: University of Pittsburgh Press, 1985).

3. (New York: Praeger Publishers for CSIS, 1997).

Part I

INTRODUCTION

1

CIVIL SOCIETY, DEMOCRACY, AND CORPORATISM IN THE THIRD WORLD

Many countries of the Third World have not in the past been very liberal; instead, they have for most of their recent histories been corporatist and often authoritarian. Whereas liberalism means a system of free and unfettered associability, pluralism, and largely unregulated interest group or nongovernmental organization (NGO) activity (what we now call civil society), corporatism (not to be equated with one of its variants, fascism) means state regulation and control of interest group/NGO activity and even the creation of official, state-run associational life.

Now as the economies of many Third World countries are being deregulated, and as authoritarianism is giving way to democracy, numerous societies and political systems are similarly transitioning from corporatism to free association, civil society, and greater societal and political pluralism. But in many countries that process is still incomplete and partial. There are often still limits on NGO/nonprofit sector (NPS) activities. Or the new groups must compete, often unfairly, with official, state-sponsored organizations. There is fear in many developing countries that unfettered, unregulated interest-group activity will produce chaos and breakdown. Many governments, while dismantling corporatism formally, are nevertheless continuing its practices; or, even though repudiating corporatism at the national level, governments are re-creating corporatist controls at the local level—precisely where many NGOs and the NPS operate. There is a delicate balance between wanting democracy and pluralism, and the reality that many Third World countries may unravel, break down, and prove ungovernable if that process proceeds too rapidly.

Liberalism and free associability have not been the sole, inevitable, or universal outcome of recent modernization processes; instead, corporatism and various mixed forms of state control/freedom have predominated. But while economic reform and democratization (parties and elections) have received a great deal of attention from scholars, policy makers, and the NGO/NPS civil society community, almost no one is analyzing the equally important phenomenon of the transition in the interest-group arena from corporatism to free associability. For if democracy is to flourish beyond the mere formal level, free, unfettered associability, genuine social and political pluralism, and civil society must also be encouraged, enhanced, and nurtured. If we are wise, that transition can be managed smoothly; if we are not, it can produce upheaval, instability, fragmentation, and a likely return to authoritarianism.

This book explores the political processes involved as Third World societies transition from authoritarianism and statism to democracy, and from corporatism to free associability. It is specifically focused on the legacy and frequently still present reality of state or government controls over NGO/civil society activity during the transition process. The research not only examines these controls in an academic sense, but it is also interested in the practical policy implications: how can the dismantling of corporatism be speeded up (if that is what is needed) and made more complete; how can we be sensitive to local mores, institutions, and ways of doing things during the crucial transitional stage; how can NGOs/NPS operate more effectively in the transitional phases and in the interstices between corporatism and liberalism or democracy; what can be done when governments seek to re-establish statist controls either at national or local levels;

how can civil society be made more effective and democracy, therefore, hopefully strengthened?

The project involves research on state controls over civil society/NGO activities in a number of key, Third World countries, consultations with NGO/NPS officials, and interviews with U.S. AID (Agency for International Development) and other U.S. government officials.

POLICY FOCUS AND AUDIENCE

This is a critically important project on an important policy issue. The author's interviews indicate that few persons in the NGO/NPS/civil society community, or in policy making in the United States government (USG) or international agencies, have sufficient background on corporatism to understand, let alone deal with in a policy sense, this phenomenon. The assumption usually is that, since Marxism-Leninism has been discredited and authoritarianism in many countries undermined, democratic, pluralist, civil society will automatically and universally follow. But the issues and processes are not so simple. The process is not necessarily inevitable, unilinear, or universal. There are many gaps, glitches, overlaps of traditional and modern, and halfway houses *between* corporatism and free associability. The Tocquevillian model of multiple, *laissez-faire* associability that is at the heart of American political and public life does not apply, or applies only partially and in mixed form, in much of the Third World.

For NGO/NPS/civil society agencies to be effective in the Third World, and particularly in countries now undergoing transitions, they must understand the context in which they are operating and be prepared to adapt their universalist programs to local, national, or regional conditions. Numerous earlier reform programs aimed at the Third World—agrarian reform, community development, family planning, judicial reform, and others—have foundered by failing to adapt to the social, political, and cultural conditions in which they found themselves. At present, however, many NGO/NPS/civil society sector leaders, although buoyed by early success of democratization, are increasingly frustrated by their inability to expand their programs. Or they are facing hurdles caused either by the reassertion of state controls or by the reluctance of Third World leaders to go faster or further toward a free society. Or they are encountering newfound hostility or increased host government suspicion, regulation, and controls over their own activities. Some NGOs have been booted out of the countries in which they were operating; others have been forced to curtail their activities; still others have been obliged to accept increased scrutiny of their finances, foreign connections, memberships, and internal procedures—that is, a reassertion of corporatism.

This research seeks to assist the NGO/NPS/civil society community in dealing with and overcoming these new restrictions and in understanding the political processes involved. In order to function effectively, NGOs must comprehend how Third World governments, fearing unrest and instability, are extremely hesitant to move to unfettered freedom of association, use the process of regulation and licensing of civil society groups to control and/or co-opt them, and try to incorporate rising social groups under official state auspices. The result is that NGOs must often navigate very carefully in these waters so as to remain effective, avoid being shunted aside into irrelevance or expulsion, and continue advancing their agenda.

The research reported here is, therefore, directed at these audiences: the NGO/NPS/civil society community, which is often not fully aware of corporatism's continuing and pervasive influences and implications in many Third World areas, U.S. policy makers in AID and other development agencies who must deal with the same phenomena, and scholars and agencies concerned with democratic transitions—such agencies as the National Endowment for Democracy (NED), National Democratic Institute for International Affairs (NDI), and National Republican Institute for International Affairs (NRI), who must wrestle with these issues. We all need to keep the goal in mind of a democratic, pluralist system of free associability, but to operate effectively we need to recognize and deal realistically with the various transitional regimes, the mixed systems involved, and the various steps or halfway houses along the way.

BACKGROUND AND MAIN QUESTIONS

In much of the theoretical literature on developing nations as well as in policy analysis, three main routes to development were usually posited: an authoritarian route, a liberal-pluralist route, and a Marxist-Leninist one.[1] Authoritarianism has been vanquished in many countries and now, with the end of the Cold War and the demise of the Marxist-Leninist alternative, it is generally thought that liberalism and pluralism will triumph universally. That may still happen in the long term, but in the meantime analysts, activists, and policy makers alike have largely ignored or not been cognizant of the other great systems outcome and alternative, particularly attractive in the unstable political systems of the Third World: corporatism.

Corporatism, organicism, and integralism, as we see in Chapter 3, have a long history in Western thought as well as political practice. Corporatism was particularly attractive in those key Third World countries (Egypt, Indonesia, Iran, South Korea, Taiwan, Brazil, Mexico) where political elites favored economic development but were often fearful of its social and political consequences (pluralism and democracy). Hence, they erected elaborate corporate structures of institutions and regulations to control, manage, co-opt, and even suppress the rising new social forces: organized labor, peasant groups, women, indigenous elements, neighborhood- and community-based groups, NGOs of all kinds, social movements, and civil society generally.

In the past two decades, as the Johns Hopkins University Center for Civil Society Studies publications emphasize,[2] there has been an explosion *worldwide* of civil society, NGOs, and private interest associations in general. In addition, particularly in the last decade, many developing nations have reformed, privatized, and moved toward neoliberalism in the economic sphere. And though many have moved toward electoral democracy, genuine liberal and pluralist democracy has proved more difficult and elusive. Many Third World nations, fearing disorder and breakdown, are reluctant to let go of the political strings, to relax or eliminate entirely the vast web of corporative regulatory controls that still remain in place. The result is a mishmash of confusion and contradictions with NGO/NPS/civil society groups and advocates caught in the middle, uncertain as to how to operate. Although a handful of developing nations have abolished corporative controls as part of a broader democratization strategy, in most the corporative controls remain in place, or else official interest associations and accompanying regulatory mechanisms exist alongside and in a conflicting, overlapping, *competitive* relationship with the newer groups and NGOs oriented toward free associability.

This research explores some fundamental questions that must be addressed by the emerging NGO/NPS/civil society/policy community:

1. What is the theoretical, sociological, and political basis of the systems of corporatism that are so widespread in the Third World but are almost entirely unknown (including among the leaders of international NGOs seeking to operate in these countries) in the United States?

2. What are the *processes* and dynamics by which corporatist systems are now being dismantled or giving way to more liberal systems of free associability; how extensive are the remaining controls on free associations; what kind of mixed systems exist, how do they change, and how do NGO/NPS/civil society groups learn to navigate around these controls?

3. What regulations and controls (legal, constitutional, political) must NGO/NPS/civil society groups still conform to and how does that inhibit their activities? What can be done to ameliorate these restrictions?

4. How can the international community (IC) and NGOs in particular assist the process of devolution from corporatist to genuinely liberal, open, and pluralist societies and politics? How can the IC put pressure on countries to deregulate NGO activity, as they are already deregulating economic activity, and move more quickly to a system of free associability?

5. In the present context, corporatism is being dismantled in many countries at the national level but recreated at the local level—precisely where many NGOs operate; how best can NGOs and civil society groups resist, work around, or reverse this tendency?

6. How can American-based NGOs in particular, in their enthusiasm for free and democratic pluralism, avoid pushing Third World countries too far and too fast in this area, and thus causing the very instability and chaos that having a strong civil society infrastructure is designed to prevent?

7. Can American NGOs and civil society advocates understand forms of civil society other than our own and thus develop the empathy necessary to deal with Third World countries on their own terms rather than through the narrow, particular lenses of U.S. pluralism and free associability?

Four types of methodologies are employed in this research. The first is dialogue, consultation, and interaction with NGO/NPS/civil society leaders and managers in the United States and the Third World to identify problems, needs, and issues as *they* perceive them. The second is library and archival research on *distinct systems* of civil society and state-society relations, and on the persistence/elimination of corporative control mechanisms in the Third World. This will involve research on constitutions, legal restrictions, political culture, and political and bureaucratic controls by which Third World governments seek to oversee and regulate NGO/NPS/civil society activities. The third method is interviewing of NGO leaders, government representatives, AID officials, and NPS officials in the case study countries. The fourth method is participant observation in a number of representative Third World countries where the issue of corporative controls over NGO activity versus free association has been particularly acute.

The research takes a broad, global view, and I have studied, worked, and traveled in all regions analyzed in Part III. But one cannot be an expert in everything and, therefore, while retaining a regional focus, I have focused on certain key countries (1) where the corporatism/control versus liberalism/free associability debate and dynamic have been especially controversial and/or unstable; (2) which are representative of their regions; and/or (3) which are especially important countries. These are Brazil and Mexico in Latin America, Egypt in the

Middle East, Taiwan and South Korea in Asia, and South Africa in Africa.

NOTES

1. For an overview, see Howard J. Wiarda, *An Introduction to Comparative Politics: Concepts and Processes* (Fort Worth: Harcourt Brace, second edition, 1999).

2. See especially the work of Lester M. Salamon and his colleagues at the Center for Civil Society Studies, Johns Hopkins University, such as *The Civil Society Sector*, *The Rise of the Nonprofit Sector*, and *Social Origins of Civil Society*.

Part II

THEORY AND CONCEPTS

2

CIVIL SOCIETY
History and Meaning(s)

The concept of civil society has a long and distinguished history in Western political thought and practice.[1] And therein, right at the beginning, lies the first and most important set of issues with which we must deal: (1) while civil society is indisputably part of the Western tradition, its meaning and implications have varied enormously over time, in different historical contexts, and from country to country; and (2) while civil society is tied to and closely a part of the distinctively Western tradition, with its emphasis at least in modern times on individualism, absence of feudal or semifeudal restraints, freedom of association, liberty, participatory and pluralist politics, and middle-class, entrepreneurial, and free-market economics, we must question whether and how much it has relevance in many Third World countries with their quite different histories, cultures, societies, economies, and political traditions. Or is civil society now such a genuinely universal concept that it is applicable to all countries in approximately the same form? Those are the issues we wrestle with in this chapter.

In this brief discussion, we cannot review the entire history of Western political thought, or even the concept of civil society in great detail within that tradition. But we do need to indicate the main trends—and the diversity of formulations within this history—in order to provide background and context for the main themes of this study.

For the ancient Greeks, where the concept received its initial systematic treatment, civil society was conceived as a commonwealth of the politically organized citizens.[2] Within this commonwealth, organized as the Greek city-state, the "civil" part of civil society referred not so much to good manners but instead to the requirements of citizenship: knowledge, discourse, participation. But already in these initial formulations we begin to see differences. Plato's conception of good citizenship was driven by his desire to set forth an inflexible, top-down, ethical base for public life that would be articulated by his "philosopher-kings"; civil society would thus be subordinated to state authority and the moral imperatives of its presumably enlightened (but unelected) leaders. In contrast, Plato's student Aristotle, more of an empiricist, recognized that life takes place at multiple associational or pluralist (civil society) levels and urged that these associations be incorporated into the political life, even while remaining committed to an ethical concept of citizenship. Right away in the founding Greek system of thought, therefore, we have two contrasting conceptions of civil society: one, state-centered, top-down, and authoritative if not authoritarian; the other, more pluralist, participatory, and consultative. Recall that in both of these ancient conceptions, however, society was viewed nondemocratically as hierarchical, with a "natural" slave class and restricted citizenship.

The Roman Empire similarly countenanced slavery, saw society as hierarchically organized, and severely restricted citizenship. Rome is honored in the Western tradition for its republicanism, but we must also recognize that it was in the Roman Empire that a full-blown system of statist corporatism came into existence for the first time.[3] By corporatism we mean a system of *state*-sponsored, *state*-licensed, *state*-organized, and *state*-controlled interest associations; representation and consultation, therefore, are also corporate, group-centered, or functionally organized, not democratically or by the principle of one person, one vote. But a state-controlled system of civil society is not what most Americans or American foreign policy makers have in mind by that term; on the other hand, we ought to recognize that in much of the Third World, and especially that part of it (most of Africa, the Middle East, and especially Latin America) influenced by the Roman law tradition, it is the corporatist and statist conception of civil society that prevails, not the free-wheeling, quasi-anarchic, unlimited pluralism of American interest-group liberalism.

Following the fall of Rome, Christianity provided the main categories of social and political life (what there was thereof) throughout the Middle ("Dark") Ages for approximately a thousand years, and for almost five hundred years longer in Southern Europe, Latin America, and large parts of Central and Eastern Europe. There are, of course, distinct emphases, nuances, and eventually quite basic differences within Christianity regarding civil society over this millennium as we move from Augustine (who condemned the classical tradition as pagan and un-Christian, emphasized man's depravity, and urged that human and societal effort be guided by moral action) to Thomas Aquinas, whose voluminous, rigorous, and highly influential writings provided the main bases for social and political organization in Christian/Catholic societies until at least World War II.[4]

Aquinas emphasized, among other things, "the great chain of being" by which all groups are both secure and fixed (locked into) in their station in life, the organic, integral, corporative, and hierarchical structure of society and politics, and the obligations of citizens to obey even while rulers were obliged to rule justly and in accord with God's commands. The proper balance between authority on the one hand and the "rights" (*fueros* in Spanish, meaning group rights) of the corporate groups (religious orders, military orders, guilds, etc.) that made up society on the other constituted for a long time (and continuing in some quarters) the accepted definition of democracy in Iberia and Latin America. Note the conception of civil society here was both corporative (statist, not liberal) and group-centered (not individualistic).

With the great sixteenth-century Jesuit (and intellectual architect of the Spanish state system in Latin America) Francisco Suárez, the still-primitive form of contract theory—rulers receive their power from God but they must rule justly—found in Aquinas was converted into a system of "prior consent" under which, in some murky past or "state of nature," the ruled had presumably given their consent to the monarch to rule in an absolute manner and act on behalf of the people and their corporate interests. This formulation has long served as a rationale for absolute monarchy or, later, political authoritarianism since it endowed the state and its ruler with near-absolute and virtually unlimited power, unencumbered by elections or any institutional means to revise the social contract once arrived at and the prior consent given.

Aquinas and the sixteenth-century neoscholastics had also helped revive Aristotelian logic, the Greek-Roman idea of a "natural" slave class (handy when confronted with the indigenous populations of Latin America), and the understanding that society required a moral, God-given base; civil society was thus constituted by religion and only Christians could be a part of it. Such an exclusionary, hierarchical, and fixed system of civil society could not last permanently in the West—except perhaps in Spain, Portugal, and their colonial offshoots in Latin America. It is significant, therefore, that political theory in "the West," including that regarding civil society, went on from the Thomistic mold to other formulations, but in Iberia and Latin America it was the Thomistic-Suárezian theory and sociology (now largely forgotten elsewhere) that continued to dominate. This tradition of thought, which eventually serves as the basis for an updated Catholic corporatism, has not only been lost or ignored in the history of Western thought but it is also largely unknown by today's civil society advocates. Nevertheless, it remains essential for an understanding of Latin America.

As we move into the modern age, a greater diversity of conceptions of civil society begins to emerge—and, recall, here we are still talking only about the Western tradition. Modernity came, among other ways, in the form of an emerging capitalism, centralizing nation-states, and in a handful of countries greater impetus to political freedom. As John Ehrenberg emphasizes, civil society was no longer understood necessarily as a universal Christian commonwealth but came to focus more on individual interest, state power, representative rule, the rule of law, and an economic order emphasizing property. Machiavelli's amoral *The Prince*[5] made him the first "modern" (secular) political scientist, but his preoccupation with power, a strong state, and the achievement of national unity left little room for civil society outside of central state control. The discovery of individual, as distinct from group, rights largely emerged from the sixteenth-century Protestant Reformation, but over time, as conflict between Catholics and Protestants spread, each prince was given free reign to choose his subjects' religion and to organize civil society (or not organize it) in his domain as he saw fit.

With Thomas Hobbes's *Leviathan* (1651)[6] we have the appearance of a new calculating individual interested mainly in his own self-interest who also had to take into account the interests of other calculating, self-interested parties. To Hobbes, civil society was not "natural" as it was in Aristotle and Aquinas but an artificial creation of the state. The state shaped, organized, and even created civil society as it saw fit and depending on political circumstances and pressure-group politics. In Hobbes's ruthless state of nature, this state-organized system of civil society provided a way to ensure peace and security, but it was a means to an end and had no independent existence of its own. As in much of the Third World today, it was state power that was dominant while civil society was subordinated to it, a means to provide a degree of popular participation but under state auspices and control.

With John Locke (1689)[7] we begin to arrive at the present American conception of civil society, but it is important to emphasize preliminarily (1) his was only one conception among many in the Western political tradition, (2) some areas (Southern and Eastern Europe, Latin America) either lagged behind or were already settled into non-Lockean (Thomistic, Suárezian) traditions, and (3) we have still not yet begun to talk about non-Western conceptions of civil society. For Locke, in contrast to Hobbes, civil society was voluntary, individualistic (not group-oriented), participatory (not created and manipulated by either the monarch or the state), and nascently democratic.

The basis of civil society was constituted by private property ("estate" in Locke's terms), the rule of law, and democratic participation. Civil society groups came together voluntarily to limit absolute rule and to preserve liberty, order, and estate.

Absolute rule would also be limited by property rights and an independent civic consciousness. Civil society thus meant the possibility of participatory citizens living together in a condition of protected property rights providing for economic prosperity and political freedom guaranteed by regular, constitutional procedures and the rule of *law.* The Lockean conception, therefore, serves as a precursor to the Madisonian idea of competing, counterbalanced interest groups ("modern" civil society) with which we are all familiar. And then with Adam Smith we have the added ingredient, fundamental to both longtime assumptions of the American foreign aid program as well as to our understanding of economic and, hence, political development in the Third World, that civil society is both an economic as well as a political system, that it is shaped and dominated by a market-oriented system of production, that freedom is required in both the economic (free markets) and political (free associability) spheres, and that it is economic growth that drives political development and constitutes the essential base before democratic civil society is possible.

Although Locke was probably the most important political theorist in the Anglo-American tradition, other traditions and conceptions of civil society emerged on the European continent. On the one hand, we have Montesquieu, close to the English aristocratic tradition, who stood for a balanced constitution, separation of powers, limits on royal absolutism, and, most importantly for our purposes, the defense of intermediary associations that helped undergird Madison's conception in the U.S. Constitution of countervailing, limiting civil society and pluralism.

But on the other, we have Rousseau, manifestly *hostile to all forms* of civil society, whose influence on Latin America and on revolutionary regimes more generally was enormous.[8] Unlike Locke, Montesquieu, or Madison, Rousseau was hardly interested in the processes of and institutions of government (elections, checks and balances, etc.). Instead, he presented a "great and glorious" vision, a secular, updated, and "enlightened" (also rather romantic) version of the earlier Christian synthesis. Rousseau's vision was of the *instant*, *spontaneous* eruption of liberty, unencumbered by institutional restraints or by the gradual, incremental training in democracy and self-government that Locke and Madison recognized as necessary. This explosion of freedom would be led by a heroic, charismatic leader who presumably knew (without the benefit of elections) and embodied the troubling concept that Rousseau brought to prominence, the "general will." Every subsequent dictator, strong man, or revolutionary elite in history, whether Augusto Pinochet on the right or Fidel Castro on the left, whether Franco, Salazar, or various military *juntas* on the one hand or the Nicaraguan Sandinistas on the other, has admired Rousseau for providing justification to those who presumably *know* the general will without having to go through the "inconvenience" of democratic elections, who can leap over the stages and long training in self-government that more realistic theorists like Locke knew were necessary, to arrive immediately at some preconceived revolutionary goal.

In this formulation Rousseau would necessarily be hostile to independent civil society, since that would constitute a limit on the general will and an obstacle to heroic revolution and the singular expression of a presumably informed consciousness. One can see, therefore, why Rousseau would be inspirational for Third World independence and revolutionary movements since he held out the promise of an immediate, uncontested leapfrogging into modernity without any training or background in democracy. Traditional political culture, the absence of institutional infrastructure, and what later political scientists called the "preconditions" for both democracy and economic growth could all be quite magically overcome by the leader who personified the general will. Rousseau (not Locke, Jefferson, or Madison) was thus not only the intellectual inspiration of the Latin American independence movements of the early nineteenth century but his influence today pervades virtually all areas of Latin American political life that have an effect (largely negative) on the growth (or lack thereof) of civil society: strong executives, weak legislatures and courts, weak local government, centralized ministries and an administrative state rather than a participatory one, absence of checks and balances, weak societies and limited associational life, and justifications for "strong government" often at the expense of human rights.

Moreover, it is not just in Latin America that these characteristics are present, although Rousseau's influence has been the longest and strongest there, but throughout the Third World and wherever Lockean, often prosaic, democratic institutions are weak. One additional note, and that is that Marx was in this sense also a "child" of Rousseau since Marx was at least equally hostile to civil society, seeing it as an agency of the bourgeoisie and as an obstacle to revolutionary change that had to be overcome and destroyed. It is no accident that all revolutionary regimes, Rousseauian or Marxian, thus seek to abolish any kind of independent civil society, substituting in its place only those officially sanctioned groups of youth, peasants, workers, women, etc., who are loyal to the revolution.

The German tradition of civil society was very different from the English or the French, the latter of which after 1789 seemed to oscillate between statist models, on the one hand, and Rousseauian popular explosions, on the other. In the German tradition, which we identify with Kant and Hegel, there is a powerful emphasis on law and order, which also required a strong state. But the state also needed to be law-governed as a way of reconciling individual moral autonomy with the need for public order. Neither Kant nor Hegel was attracted to American-style individualism or the "anarchy" of a *laissez-faire* marketplace, either in the economic or the political spheres; rather, they emphasized the need for a system of laws and regulations and a bureaucratic state. They feared the chaos that they saw inherent in Locke's, Smith's, or Madison's conception of the autonomous, unfettered individual and of societal-political pluralism; they favored instead a well-ordered state governed by law and administrative procedures. As Ehrenberg puts it, there could be no freedom without law, no civil society without a strong state, and no social peace without administration coupled with the threat of coercion.[9]

With Tocqueville,[10] we now go back to the United States and perhaps the quintessential expression of the American infatuation, romance, and (currently official) policy regarding civil society. Alexis de Tocqueville was a French intellectual and aristocrat who visited America in the 1830s and whose *Democracy in America* is universally recognized as one of (if not *the*) best analysis of American society and politics ever done. What most impressed this perceptive visitor was the incredible strength of intermediate associations or civil society in America, those groups that lie between the individual and the state, that serve as transmission belts for conveying private interest concerns to government decision makers and back down again as implementers of public policy, that help to mediate between state and citizen, and that serve both as expressions of popular sentiment and as limits on arbitrary government.

Tocqueville was particularly admiring of the New England town meeting, but he lauded other forms of intermediary associations and associational life in general. Tocqueville saw these associations as both the underpinning and the genius of American democracy since he recognized that they fused (the age-old dilemma of all political systems) order and liberty as well as private interest and the common good. In modern times, Tocqueville's arguments would be elaborated and updated in what in political science is called interest-group pluralism or interest-group liberalism, which author Theodore Lowi has called *the* American political ideology.[11] And it is precisely this feature, now referred to as civil society, that America and its nongovernmental organizations seek to export abroad, that has become a, or perhaps *the,* cornerstone of America's democracy initiatives in other countries, and that we would like to assume is part of a global, universal, civil society movement.

But is it? Is civil society really a universal concept or is it particularly American, a product of our particular history, frontiers, absence of feudalism, open society, culture, economy, and historically wide-open spaces? Can civil society be successfully exported to other countries where the history, culture, socioeconomic structures, role of the state, etc., are so much different from our own?

In this brief survey of the history of Western thought with regard to civil society, we have already discovered not only a sometimes bewildering array of definitions and formulations of civil society but also of entire, quite different national and regional traditions shaped by distinct ideas of the state-society relationship. In Plato's formulation, civil society was subordinated to the enlightened, top-down views of his philosopher-kings, whereas Aristotle was more sympathetic to the civil society basis of politics. The Romans emphasized corporate group over individual rights, while Aquinas made Christianity the basis for all society. Machiavelli and Hobbes subordinated civil society to the state, whereas Locke and Madison subordinated the state to civil society. Rousseau and Marx were hostile to civil society if it interfered with their revolutionary goals, while Tocqueville and modern American interest-group theorists celebrated it.

Then, there are the distinct national and regional traditions: the Christian-Thomistic conception of Catholic Europe, Latin America, and the Philippines; the Anglo-American tradition whose apostle is Locke; the French tradition(s) of elitism on the one hand and Rousseau (also extremely popular in the Third World) on the other; the German tradition of law, administration, and bureaucracy; the Russian tradition, whether under the czars or the Bolsheviks, of absolute central authority; and the American conception of virtually anarchic, unfettered interest-group pluralism.

These varying conceptions are all still within the Western tradition; the constellation of diverse meanings and traditions of civil society and state-society relations is compounded if we move to the non-West.[12] Japan's economy is the world's second most powerful; its per-capita income ranks it as one of the world's richest; and its political system is stable and functional. Yet its civil society is inordinately weak compared to other developed, democratic countries with little apparent loss to the dynamic, highly developed rhythms and quality of Japanese life. China and other East Asian countries cast in the Confucian mold have achieved remarkable, even miracle economic growth rates under strong, centralized, bureaucratic governments seemingly without, until recently, the presence of strong civil society.

In contrast, India has a strong civil society but its economic performance has been far more feeble than these others; in addition, when we speak of civil society in India, we are in considerable measure talking about caste associations, and I am not sure these ascriptive, racist, traditionalist (although now often performing modern functions) institutions are what its advocates have in mind when they speak of civil society.[13]

In the predominantly Muslim countries, and outside of them, there is a great debate as to whether Islam and democracy are compatible; and though there is no express prohibition either in the *Koran* or the *Shariah* against democracy or civil society, certainly the Islamic tradition has not been supportive of either of these concepts or the institutions of democracy that go with them. In Sub-Saharan Africa, democracy, social structures, and political systems are all under severe, perhaps mortal threat; what there is of civil society is largely found in ethnic or tribal groups and, as with India's caste associations, that traditional, parochial institution may not be the kind of civil society that the concept's advocates wish to see. Finally, in Latin America we have one of the most complex situations: an incredible mix, jumble, and perhaps dysfunctional hodgepodge of earlier Christian, Thomistic conceptions of civil society, Enlightenment and "rationalist" Rousseauian forms, and statist and corporatist forms, coupled with nascently American-style pluralism.

This survey of the history and theory of civil society highlights (1) how ambiguous the concept is, (2) how its meaning has varied over time and from one country or culture to another, (3) the incredible diversity of civil society corresponding to the diversity of the world's political systems, and (4) that civil society exists in both democratic and participatory forms as well as in nondemocratic and not-so-benign forms. The problem for policy is that civil society advocates, mainly American, have latched onto and adopted one particular form, the pleasantly liberal Lockean-Madisonian-Tocquevillian-Rooseveltian form, assumed that form is universal, and sought to export it to the rest of the world. But that form of civil society is in fact uniquely American; it is not universal; it cannot be effectively exported to other nations and cultures whose histories and traditions are fundamentally different from our own; and, therefore, instead of producing democracy and stability, these efforts may serve to perpetuate corporatism on the one hand, or produce instability, fragmentation, and national breakdown on the other—just the opposite of the effects intended by civil society advocates.

In much of the literature on civil society it is assumed that, above and beyond the national, regional, and distinct cultural traditions described here, there are only three extant forms of civil society: the Marxist-Leninist, the authoritarian, and the liberal-democratic. But Marxism-Leninism has now been vanquished; authoritarianism has similarly been in retreat in various parts of the globe; and that should leave only the liberal-democratic. In other words, with the decline and disappearance of the other two alternatives, liberal democracy should now have the playing field all to itself since it is "the only game in town"; the Third World should now be a kind of *tabula rasa* ("blank page") on which civil society advocates can now impose their vision quite literally at will. But that ignores (1) the still-powerful force of indigenous institutions and ways of doing things in many Third World countries, (2) the enormous confusion present (as in Latin America) because of the incredible overlap, fusion, and crazy-quilt patterns of conflicting crosscurrents of different civil society conceptions, and (3) the still-powerful presence of a fourth great "ism" in addition to the other three mentioned, one that is almost entirely unknown in foreign aid agencies and among civil society advocacy groups, and that is *corporatism*. It is to that subject that the analysis now turns.

NOTES

1. John Ehrenberg, *Civil Society: The Critical History of an Idea* (New York: New York University Press, 1999); Ernest Gellner, *Conditions of Liberty: Civil Society and Its Rivals* (New York: Penguin, 1994).

2. The analysis in the historical section follows that of Ehrenberg.

3. W. W. Buckland, *A Text Book of Roman Law from Augustus to Justinian* (Cambridge: Cambridge University Press, 1966).

4. Otto Gierke, *Political Theories of the Middle Ages* (Cambridge: Harvard University Press, 1987).

5. (New York: Penguin, 1961).

6. (New York: Penguin, 1985).

7. John Locke, *Two Treaties on Government* (New York: Cambridge University Press, 1960).

8. Jean-Jacques Rousseau, *On the Social Contract* (New York: St. Martin's, 1978).

9. Ehrenberg, *Civil Society*, p. 117.

10. Alexis de Tocqueville, *Democracy in America* (New York: Random House, 1990).

11. Theodore Lowi, *The End of Liberalism: Ideology, Policy, and the Crisis of Public Authority* (New York: Norton, 1969).

12. Howard J. Wiarda (ed.), *Non-Western Theories of Development* (Fort Worth: Harcourt Brace, 1999); and Wiarda (ed.), *Comparative Democracy and Democratization* (Fort Worth: Harcourt Brace, 2001).

13. Lloyd Rudolph and Susan Rudolph, *The Modernity of Tradition* (Chicago: University of Chicago Press, 1967).

3

CORPORATIST
SYSTEMS OF CIVIL SOCIETY

Of all the great "isms" of the modern world—socialism, capitalism, liberalism, fascism, totalitarianism—the one that is least well known is corporatism.[1] Or else, as is sometimes done, we associate corporatism with fascism and assume that it disappeared in the defeat of the Axis powers in World War II.

In fact, corporatism is very much alive and well in various parts of the world. It is present in its pluralist, democratic, participatory, and "societal" form, in the system of institutionalized cooperation and incorporation of interest groups into the decision making of the modern state, in much of Europe, Japan, even North America. It is at least equally prevalent in the Third World, particularly in East and Southeast Asia, Latin America, the Middle East, and Sub-Saharan Africa, in more statist, bureaucratic, top-down, and controlling forms. The decline or disappearance of many authoritarian regimes in the Third World has often led us to believe that corporatism disappeared along with them; but, in fact, though manifest or ideological corporatism *has* in many countries been replaced by a form of often quite limited ("illiberal," "delegative," "controlled") democracy, corporatism's control mechanisms to regulate interest-group activity have very often been kept in place. Indeed, it is the very persistence, in whole or in part, of these corporatist control mechanisms that largely explains why the new democracies of the Third World are so often limited and illiberal, and why the so-called "second stage" or "second generation" reforms—transparency, judicial reform, etc.—promoted by democracy advocates have so far, in most countries, failed to go very far.

But if democracy and civil society advocates wish to see their agenda advanced, they must, in one way or another, come to grips with the corporatism phenomenon. Either corporatism has to be completely dismantled (unlikely) for full democracy to emerge or it has to be lived with and accommodated. Whichever policy option is adopted, it is plain that corporatism as an ongoing, omnipresent political phenomenon has to be dealt with realistically. And before we are able to do that, we had better be clear as to what corporatism is and how it operates.

THE POLITICAL THEORY AND TRADITION OF CORPORATISM

Corporatism may be defined as a system of social and political organization in which the state controls, limits, sometimes monopolizes, even *creates* the interest-group life or "civil society" that swirls about it. Particularly as societies begin to modernize and become more pluralistic, corporatist control mechanisms often look very attractive to ruling elites, both military and civilian (corporatism is thus compatible with elected governments), as a means of harnessing the often disruptive social forces and inevitable pluralism that accompanies modernization. Corporatism is thus employed because it allows for economic growth and social development but without those unleashing potentially destabilizing political forces. Corporatist controls over social and political groups may be considered at the opposite end of the spectrum of liberal, pluralist, free associability, or democracy; and most countries are strung out along this spectrum with varying degrees of corporatism versus liberalism.

In the literature, distinctions are made between "natural" corporatism and "manifest" corporatism, and between "societal" corporatism and "state" corporatism. Natural corporatism tends to occur in societies whose historic political and cultural premises tend to be organic, integral, and communitarian (e.g., Japan, China, many Catholic countries; not the United States); manifest corporatism is imposed from above, bureaucratically, by the state, often dictatorially (Mussolini's Italy, Franco's Spain), though it should be said that manifest corporatism most often occurs in countries that also have a natural-corporatist tradition. State corporatism is similarly imposed from the top down and is usually authoritarian, whereas societal corporatism tends to emerge from the bottom up, from grassroots levels, and may be a product of religious or cultural communalism and is not incompatible with democracy.

The concept of corporatism has a long tradition in Western political theory, organization, and practice—as long as that of civil society, with whose history it is closely entwined.[2] Like civil society, corporatism has its origins in the ancient world of Greece and Rome. Greece was organized on a corporatist, group, or "functional" basis both vertically (in terms of classes) and horizontally (by occupations: soldiers, priests, artisans, craftsmen); representation was similarly on a group or corporatist basis rather than on the basis of individualism or, as we now put it, one person, one vote. Rome continued this system of sectoral or functional representation in its republic but on the much larger basis of *empire,* as compared with the Greek city-state; Rome also formulated a far more elaborate system of corporate group rights and responsibilities, as well as internal or self and state policing, regulation, and superintendency of group activity.

The Christian conception of the Middle Ages, particularly in Thomas Aquinas and his followers, continued this group or communitarian orientation but, of course, emphasized that it was a Christian community. In Aquinas's great chain of being, each individual as well as each group was secure in his/her station in life as a member of God's holy family—the family being the primary and most basic corporate group in society. Society was organized hierarchically (God, angels, archangels, etc., eventually down to men—rulers, leaders, artisans, servants, slaves) as well as vertically into its component corporate units (religious orders, military orders, towns, guilds, and so on).

In the later Middle Ages this would grow into a system of estates (nobility, religious, common) as well as, in many European countries, an emerging system of representation and consultation that was also corporately, group-, or estate-based.[3] As modern nation-states began to emerge from the fourteenth century on, their political dynamics and institutions were importantly shaped by the ongoing struggle between the centralizing, controlling tendencies of royal authority and the effort at preserving autonomy, self-governance, and local independence on the part of corporate entities. The outcome could be either limited monarchy and some degree of representative, pluralist government as in England, or the snuffing out of corporate group life and the triumph of royal absolutism as in Spain and France. One can today witness in much of the Third World, often similarly organized on a corporate or communal basis, a parallel, ongoing struggle between central state government seeking to rationalize and control the national political life, and the associational and group life (civil society) that seeks to maintain autonomy from it. Importantly for our future considerations, the outcome of this struggle can be either authoritarianism or pluralist democracy, and all gradations in between.

The French Revolution of 1789 abolished the system of estates associated with the *ancien régime,* and also the system of corporate or group rights and obligations, in favor of the emerging idea, more or less established, of individual rights. France officially abolished the guilds and the "corporations" of the old system in 1791; many other countries in Western Europe followed suit in the first decades of the nineteenth century. But while many of these corporate agencies were *officially* abolished, de facto many of them managed to hang on and to remain influential. Depending on the country involved, the Roman Catholic Church, the Lutheran Church, many of the earlier guilds, various self-governing towns and principalities managed to hang onto their corporate rights and privileges. At the same time, such new entities in many countries as commercial or industrial associations, farm groups, or the national army acquired quasi- or actual corporate standing.

Following the French Revolution and continuing until approximately the mid-nineteenth century, the Roman Catholic Church, which had lost a great deal of property, buildings, and lives in the Revolution, turned reactionary. Recall, it was the Church and particularly Aquinas that had articulated a corporatist view of society and politics for most of the Middle Ages; now the Church sought to roll the clock back, to restore the status quo ante, to go back to the easier, "sleepier," stable social order of before 1789. But, of course, once the great motor forces of industrialization, modernization, and rapid social change had been set loose, it proved impossible to go back—witness the European revolutions of 1830 and 1848.

By midcentury the Church had begun to abandon its reactionary position. It recognized that society had changed, that it could not turn the clock back, and that it needed to deal with the new realities. The Church respects the majesty of facts. Therefore, a number of clerics and even some bishops began calling for a new, updated form of corporatism, one that included the emerging labor movement as well as the bourgeoisie. The Church was urged to address "the social question," to solve the problems of anomie, alienation, poverty, and rootlessness emerging in modern, industrial society. These were, of course, all the problems that Marx was also addressing in his *Manifesto* of 1848, and there is no doubt that Catholic corporatism was in part conceived as a way not only to head off Marxist revolution but also to reclaim territory and people already lost to Catholicism's hated rivals, Marxism as well as liberalism.[4]

By the 1880s Catholic corporatism was a growing movement. Major international conferences were convoked on the subject in 1884 and 1890. Corporatism was now explicitly defined for the first time as "a system of social organization that has as its base the grouping of men by functions, and as true and proper organs of the state they direct and coordinate labor and capital in matters of common interest." In 1891 Pope Leo XIII issued the famous encyclical *Rerum Novarum*, which provided legitimation to workers' movements and galvanized the Church to take the lead in this area.

MODERN CORPORATISM

In the decades leading up to World War I, the Church sponsored the growth of quite a number of Catholic workers' movements. Called "Workers' Circles" rather than labor movements, these organizations emerged in Italy, Spain, Belgium, France, Austria, Switzerland, and Germany. In accord with the earlier guild philosophy, these movements advocated class harmony and cooperation rather than the Marxian class struggle and conflict. At the same time they urged that both business and labor be integrated into government decision making rather than being separate from the state as under liberalism. Though most often paternalistic and controlled by clerical and business interests, the Workers' Circles grew steadily in the early twentieth century, competing with Marxist unions. The movement was referred to as "the Catholic International" to contrast it with the Marxian Socialist International.

The period between World Wars I and II was the high point for this form of Catholic corporatism. The Bolshevik Revolution of 1917 and upheavals in Germany and other countries immediately after the war threw a scare into Catholics and conservatives everywhere, prompting a Catholic revival in the 1920s that sought to recapture its flock for the Church. Then came the economic depression and political collapse in the 1930s in many countries that seemed to indicate the failure of liberalism, both economically and politically. With liberalism collapsing and Marxism unacceptable, corporatism seemed to be the only alternative. Corporatist regimes in one form or another came to power throughout Europe, in Italy, Portugal, Spain, Austria, Poland, Czechoslovakia, Hungary, Estonia, Greece, Lithuania, Romania, Bulgaria, Germany, Latvia, Belgium, and France, for varying lengths of time.

In power, corporatism proved much less attractive, effective, and even-handed than its ideology had sounded. Most of the corporatist regimes listed above proved to be authoritarian and dictatorial rather than participatory and grassroots oriented. Instead of the co-equal treatment of labor and employers, business interests usually received special treatment from the state while labor was subordinated and subjected to often harsh controls or repression. In Italy and Germany, the more-or-less democratic thrust of the earlier Catholic social movement gave way to full-scale fascism and totalitarianism. With the defeat of the Axis powers in World War II, and corporatism's identification in the popular mind with fascism, corporatism appeared to have been completely discredited; after the war, corporatism as a manifest ideology and movement seemed to all but completely disappear.[5]

But many countries, while repudiating corporatism ideologically, nevertheless continued to practice a disguised form of corporatism, even while not calling it that. That is, in the postwar period they resurrected and reconstituted systems of state-society relations that, in classic corporatist form, integrated labor and business into a tripartite relationship with the state, under which these groups were not only *consulted* (as in interest-group pluralism) on public policy but were actually incorporated into the regulatory and social programs of the modern state and became part of decision making. This form of societal, as distinct from state, corporatism was quite compatible with elections, democracy, and parliamentary government. Austria was perhaps the most "corporatized" country in this regard, followed by Sweden, Germany, the other Scandinavian countries, The Netherlands, Belgium, France, Italy, and, to a lesser degree, Great Britain. Over time a number of scholars began to discover, or perhaps rediscover, these forms of corporatism embedded in the modern, regulatory, social state and to actually call it that.[6]

Meanwhile, in Franco's Spain and Salazar's Portugal, the older forms of 1930s-style authoritarian or state corporatism, though attenuated, continued to be practiced. At the same time, in much of the developing world, now independent after long histories of colonialism, corporatism also proved attractive. This was particularly true in Africa, Asia, and Latin America, where in the late 1960s earlier democratic regimes gave way before a large wave of authoritarianism. Quite a number of Third World countries had their own indigenous forms of corporatism; others practiced bureaucratic-authoritarian control over all social and interest-group activities without knowing about or calling it that; still others actually journeyed to Spain and Portugal to find out how Franco and Salazar had done it. The "it" in this case refers to the achievement of impressive, even "miracle" economic growth during the 1960s and early 1970s by these two regimes but using corporatist structures to control and regulate interest-group activity so that economic development did not give rise to pressures for liberalism and democracy beyond a dictatorial or authoritarian government's ability to control them. Examples include Nasser's Egypt, the Shah's Iran, Suharto's Indonesia, Marcos's Philippines, the South Korean and Taiwanese regimes, almost all the new Middle Eastern and African authoritarian regimes, and seventeen of the twenty countries in Latin America. Corporatism in its authoritarian, top-down, and statist-bureaucratic forms had made a Third World *global* comeback; it was no longer confined just to Europe or to the historically Catholic countries.

One can readily understand why corporatism, whether formally called that or not, would be so attractive in these Third World modernizing regimes. First, corporatism, through its state control mechanisms, helped maintain order, stability, unity, and social peace in a time in many Third World countries of potential for disorder, instability, fragmentation, and social conflict. Second, corporatism helped these regimes secure more-or-less regular and continuous economic growth without giving way to the social pluralism and demands for democracy that such growth usually stimulates. Third, corporatism helped enable elite groups, whether civilian, military, or a combination, both to remain in power and to control, regulate, slow, and limit the process by which new (middle- and lower-class) groups were admitted to the system. Fourth, corporatism was adaptive (although in practice it proved too rigid), enabling a modernizing regime to adjust slowly to change without producing either the disruptive upheaval or chaotic revolution plaguing many Third World countries. In short, corporatism had a number of features that made it enormously attractive throughout the Third World.

Here is how the system worked in practice. Under corporatism, an elaborate system of rules and regulations was established governing labor union (and other groups, too) activities. They were required to disclose their membership lists, financing, leadership, and other details; they had to *apply* for recognition and juridical personality—unlike in liberalism where groups may function in free associability. The power to grant recognition to a group obviously carried the power to deny, postpone, or withhold recognition. If a group chose to exercise political action (strikes, demonstrations, marches) in the absence of official recognition, the regime could, by law, take police action against it. As implemented, the restrictive corporatist laws were far more enforced against change-oriented groups (labor, peasants, students) than against the business sector and other conservative groups.[7]

In fact, the process of accepting, adding, and giving legitimacy to new corporatist groups was often more dynamic than simply the use of repression. The regime in power consciously used the restrictive corporatist laws to divide the labor movement, incorporating those groups that, in return for some limited benefits for their members, agreed to go along with the restrictions, separating them from those groups that insisted on complete independence and, often, a revolutionary strategy. There were, in other words, both co-optive and coercive aspects to corporatism, both carrots and sticks. In addition, there was usually a political process involved: In the early years of social pluralism when the new groups were small and weak, authoritarian regimes often used repression to subdue them; but once a group reached a certain size and power, and repression would have to be used on a massive or totalitarian (as distinct from milder authoritarian) scale, some accommodation was frequently reached. Such an accommodation usually involved some greater benefits and the loosening of the earlier controls, in return for an agreement to refrain from disruptive strikes and violence. These agreements could be renegotiated on an almost daily basis, and obviously such an accommodation fell short of full democracy and unfettered pluralism. On the other hand, even a limited agreement provided some benefits, was far better than complete authoritarianism and full dictatorial controls, and was often a step on the way back to democracy. The South Korean and Taiwanese regimes of the 1980s are good examples of this transition from closed, authoritarian corporatism to open, more pluralist corporatism, and eventually to democracy.

By the 1980s, of course, and not just in these two countries, the swing back or "third wave" of democracy was well under way.[8] Political commentators and as social activists have simply assumed that such democratization would automatically result in free associability or uncontrolled interest-group pluralism as well. But that has not been the case. First, democratization in its initial stages in many countries was often limited to the holding of elections and some other usually modest political reforms; it did not necessarily imply interest-group freedom or, if it did, this took the form of the formal abolition of corporatism but not necessarily its practice. Second, political elites in these countries, even democratizing ones, often saw the advantages of keeping some corporatist controls in place ("in reserve") so as to serve as a useful check, if necessary, on such rapid popular mobilization in case it might prove to be disruptive and upsetting of economic growth. Third, these same elites then often created "civil society" organizations of their own, which helps explain why civil society in much of the Third World is still an elite, upper-middle-class phenomenon. The result, fourth, in most developing Third World nations, is not some quick, easy, and thoroughgoing transition from authoritarian corporatism to complete free associability, but rather an incredible confusion, mishmash, and blend of partial democracy and free associability on the one hand, and limited mobilization and the persistence of corporatist controls, either formally still in place or informally exercised in practice, on the other.

Because they do not understand corporatism well, civil society advocates do not always comprehend these transitional politics well either, which in much of the Third World is incredibly complex. On the one hand, we have the newer civil society groups organized on the basis of free associability; on the other, we have the older corporate groups. Many groups are mixed, partly free and partly controlled by and dependent on the state. These groups all compete with each other as well as in the democratic political process *and* for state attention and favors. These same groups, usually unevenly, are also connected with outside funding agencies and international civil society groups. At the same time, the state in these countries is trying to juggle all these actors and control or regulate as many as it can. Although it may have formally repealed corporatism at the national level, it often seeks to reassert corporatism informally or at regional and local levels. And though the state may still seek to control its own corporatist groups, it has a harder time—short of expelling them from the country—controlling those that are foreign-based. Meanwhile, there are dynamic factors in all of this: societies change; economies grow; new political forces and issues emerge; globalization has its effects—all of which call for a renegotiation of group relations, state power, and state-society relations.

The result is a very complex kaleidoscope of shifting political forces and constantly changing state-society relations that is far more complex than our oversimplified idea of the smooth shift from authoritarianism to democracy or from corporatism to free associability. If we wish democracy to advance and civil society to expand, we need to be aware of all these complexities.

NOTES

1. For background see Howard J. Wiarda, *Corporatism and Comparative Politics: The Other Great "Ism"* (New York: M. E. Sharpe, 1997a).

2. Karl Landauer, *Corporate State Ideologies: Historical Roots and Philosophical Origins* (Berkeley: University of California, Institute of International Studies, 1983).

3. Archibald Lewis, *The Development of Southern French and Catalan Society, 718–1050* (Austin: University of Texas Press, 1965); Angus McKay, *Spain in the Middle Ages: From Frontier to Empire, 1000–1500* (London: Macmillan, 1977).

4. Ralph Bowen, *German Theories of the Corporative State* (New York: McGraw-Hill, 1947); Matthew Elbow, *French Corporative Theory, 1789–1948* (New York: Columbia University Press, 1953).

5. Alfred Diamint, *Austria's Catholics and the First Republic* (Princeton: Princeton University Press, 1960); G. Lowell Field, *The Syndical and Corporative Institutions of Italian Fascism* (New York: Columbia University Press,

1938); Howard J. Wiarda, *Corporatism and Development: The Portuguese Experience* (Amherst: University of Massachusetts Press, 1977).

6. Samuel Beer, *Modern British Politics* (London: Faber, 1969); Andrew Shonfield, *Modern Capitalism* (London: Oxford University Press, 1965).

7. See Wiarda, *Corporatism and Comparative Politics*.

8. Samuel P. Huntington, *The Third Wave: Democratization in the Late Twentieth Century* (Norman: Oklahoma University Press, 1991).

Part III

CASE STUDIES
IN CIVIL SOCIETY

Unity and Divergence

Almost everyone supports civil society, including the present author. How could anyone be against an idea that stands for so many good things: grassroots participation, good government, democracy, and pluralism? Since everyone is in favor—at least in the abstract—the question is not whether we support or oppose civil society. Instead, the issue is the precise meaning, form, functions, priority, and institutional structure that civil society takes in different societies. The previous chapters have highlighted the distinct meanings and kinds of civil society within the Western tradition, to say nothing of the non-West, and especially focused on the attractiveness and persistence of controlled, state-structured, or corporatist forms of civil society in the developing and transitional nations. Here we expand that discussion by analyzing the distinct patterns of civil society and state-society relations in specific countries and regional areas on a global basis.

It is obvious that no one person can acquire in-depth expertise on all the world's areas and countries. On the other hand, I am just coming off a year-long sabbatical leave of extensive travel and research in Western Europe, Central and Eastern Europe, Africa, Asia, Latin America, and the Middle East. In addition, the original research proposal for this project called for a series of representative case studies in all these areas, not complete coverage. Our purpose is not to analyze all these cases in "detail" (that is reserved for a planned follow-up study) but to examine major trends, patterns, and large themes.

We look at all these areas and countries systematically in terms of four main themes or variables: (1) levels of socioeconomic development (on the assumption that there is a relationship between development and civil society), (2) the role of political culture in shaping distinct forms of civil society, (3) the changing structure or institutions of state–society relations under the impact of modernization and democratization, and (4) the international context and role of international actors in influencing civil society development and relations. We offer assessments and conclusions about each area and, overall, the strength and role of civil society.

4

SUB-SAHARAN AFRICA

Sub-Saharan Africa is the world's *least*-developed area. It is plagued by disease, misery, economic underdevelopment, high illiteracy, unstable and often repressive governments, civil war and conflict, absence of strong national institutions, lack of social safety nets, failed states, inadequate health care and doctors, ungovernability, weak institutions, mass starvation, and absence of hope.[1] Virtually every problem that one can think of associated with the vicious circles of underdevelopment is present in Africa. It also has, and as a correlate of the above, the weakest civil society of all the areas surveyed here.

SOCIOECONOMIC INDICATORS

When the World Bank and other agencies talk about the poorest of the poor, those hundreds of millions of people whose income is under $1.00 per day and who live in abject poverty, it is largely Sub-Saharan Africa that they are speaking of. Many countries of the area, as Table 4.1 shows, have an average yearly income of about $300 per person. That puts them at a level of about one one-*hundredth* of the per-capita income of the wealthy countries of North America, Western Europe, or Japan. Much of the meager wealth that does exist is squandered, terribly unevenly distributed, or finds its way into the private accounts of corrupt government and military officials.

Table 4.1   Socioeconomic Indicators, Sub-Saharan Africa

Country	GNP	GNP per capita	Life expectancy		Literacy		Urban Percent	GNP per capita rank
			Male	Female	Male	Female		
South Africa	133.2	3,160	61	66	85	84	52	86
Angola	2.7	220	45	48			34	194
Benin	2.3	381	52	55	54	23	42	165
Botswana	5.1	3,240	45	47	73	78	50	84
Burkina Faso	2.6	240	43	45	32	13	18	190
Burundi	0.8	120	41	44	55	37	9	204
Cameroon	8.5	580	53	56	80	67	48	150
Central Af. Repub.	1.0	290	43	46	49	31	23	181
Chad	1.6	200	47	50	49	31	23	196
Comoros	0.2	350	60		58			
Congo, Dem. Rep.	1.9	670	49	52	71	47	30	147
Côte d'Ivoire	10.4	710	46	47	53	36	46	146
Eritrea	0.8	200	49	52	66	38	18	196
Ethiopia	6.6	100	42	44	42	30	17	206
Gabon	4.0	3,350	53					
Gambia	0.4	340	53		35			
Ghana	7.4	390	58	62	78	60	38	164
Guinea	3.7	510	46	47			32	155
Guinea-Bissau	0.2	160	44		37			
Kenya	10.6	360	50	52	88	73	32	170
Lesotho	1.2	550	54	57	71	93	27	152
Liberia			47		51			
Madagascar	3.7	250	56	59	72	58	29	187
Malawi	2.0	190	42	42	73	44	24	199
Mali	2.6	240	49	52	46	31	29	190
Mauritania	1.0	380	52	55	52	31	56	165
Mauritius	4.2	3,590	71	84				
Mozambique	3.9	230	44	47	58	27	39	193
Niger	2.0	190	44	48	22	7	20	199
Nigeria	37.9	310	52	55	70	52	43	179
Rwanda	2.1	250	40	42	71	57	6	187
São Tomé & Principe	0.04	270	64					

Table 4.1   Socioeconomic Indicators, Sub-Saharan Africa (continued)

Country	GNP	GNP per capita	Life expectancy		Literacy		Urban Percent	GNP per capita rank
			Male	Female	Male	Female		
Senegal	4.7	510	51	54	45	26	47	155
Seychelles	0.5	6,540	72					
Sierra Leone	0.7	130	36	39	36	203		
Somalia		755 or less[a]	48					
Sudan	9.4	330	55		56			
Tanzania	8.0	240	46	48	83	64	32	190
Togo	1.5	320	47	50	72	38	33	176
Uganda	6.8	320	42	41	76	54	14	176
Zambia	3.2	320	43	43	84	69	40	176
Zimbabwe	6.1	520	50	52	92	83	35	154

SOURCE: World Bank, *World Development Report 2000–2001*. The data for some countries is missing or incomplete.

[a]Estimates by World Bank.

The poverty and misery of Sub-Saharan Africa—and part of the reason for the absence of strong civil society—may be gleaned from the accompanying table. Note that the gross national product of South Africa, the main focus of this chapter, is overwhelmingly superior to that of all other countries in the area—and roughly equivalent to all the other countries combined. On a per-person basis, only Botswana, Gabon, Mauritius, South Africa, and The Seychelles have *begun* to lift themselves out of poverty. Life expectancy in Sub-Saharan Africa is mainly in the 40- to 50-year range compared to 70–80 years in the developed countries. Literacy rates are similarly low but show considerable variation between countries. And most Sub-Saharan African countries are still predominantly rural and agricultural as compared with the more developed countries that are predominantly urban. Poverty, high illiteracy, low life expectancy, subsistence agriculture—none of these conditions is propitious for the growth of civil society and democracy. Nor do we see in Sub-Saharan Africa, of the forty-two countries listed, more than four (only 10 percent) that have had the kind of economic growth and social modernization necessary to stimulate the rise of civil society that would lead to greater pluralism and democracy (see the discussion in Chapter 5 of South Korea and Taiwan).

Because of the incredible poverty and underdevelopment, the system of civil society in Sub-Saharan Africa is generally weak, unstable, inadequately organized, and generally ineffective.[2] Of course, one must distinguish between countries, with some (Senegal, Ivory Coast, Kenya, Botswana, South Africa) having stronger civil society than others. But overall, the picture is a bleak one. Moreover, the kind of civil society that does exist is often ethnically or tribally based, a kind of organization that is usually viewed as "traditional" and is, therefore, rejected by most international aid donors. My own orientation, in contrast, is to see in these organizations a measure of hope in what seems an oftentimes hopeless situation, a way of delivering some, however limited, services (social, educational, police, justice) in a context where other civil society agencies are weak or nonexistent, and perhaps the basis for an indigenous or home-grown system of civil society. But the orientation of most civil society advocates as well as many African intellectuals and officials is to denigrate tribally based civil society as "backward," presumably to be replaced by more modern institutions. Not only is civil society weak, therefore, but many Westerners and Africans alike are not sure they like or want the form (tribal, ethnic) of civil society that does exist. And, to the extent that civil society is tribally or ethnically based, it may also be a sign of a weak or a failed state and thus not necessarily a hopeful sign of democracy. In much of the world, and certainly in the theoretical literature, civil society and democracy are closely correlated; but in Sub-Saharan Africa, with its weak, corrupt, and ineffective states, coupled with ethnically and even gang-based civil society, the correlation between democracy and civil society may be negative.[3]

ANALYSIS AND CASE STUDIES

There are two basic problems of civil society in Sub-Saharan Africa. The first, already alluded to, is the low level of social and economic development in the area, which makes the institutionalization and consolidation of *any* viable form of civil society difficult at best. Sub-Saharan Africa simply lacks the educational base, the literacy, the communications grids, the mobilized and organized populations, the webs of association life at grassroots levels, the interest group and political party systems, and the governmental infrastructure, funding support, and public policy implementing capability to develop a healthy, vibrant civil society. Civil society grows with difficulty in developed countries; its emergence is far more difficult in less-developed countries, which lack the socioeconomic underpinnings and prerequisites for it to grow.

The second reason for civil society's weakness in Sub-Saharan Africa is political: the weakness, tribulations, and *absence* in many countries of democracy.[4] Of the forty-eight countries in Sub-Saharan Africa, only eight (Botswana, Malawi, Mali, Namibia, Nigeria, Senegal, South Africa, Tanzania) embrace pluralism, are democracies, or are making a transition to democracy.

Civil society, of course, thrives best under democracy, in open countries, but in most of Africa authoritarian regimes limit, co-opt, weaken, or destroy all civil society groups that they cannot themselves control. Or they create official civil society groups—the corporatism phenomenon—by which they dominate potentially dangerous, oppositionist grassroots organizations. Civil society is unable to hold governments accountable—one of the prime purposes of civil society—if their only two alternatives are suppression or co-optation. In addition, about half the states in Sub-Saharan Africa are engaged in war, conflict, or armed disputes, both domestically and internationally. Ethnic and religious strife is also rampant, producing, especially in Central Africa, some of the world's worst cases of genocide. None of this is propitious for the growth of civil society.

In Latin America, as we see below, civil society often emerged *during* an authoritarian interlude and was a prime force in stimulating opposition to the ruling dictatorship and in the subsequent transition to democracy. But in Latin America, (1) civil society is generally stronger than it is in Sub-Saharan Africa, and (2) there was a *preexisting* civil society that could then be revived in the transition to democracy. In

Sub-Saharan Africa, however, the base for civil society is weak and there is no or little preexisting civil society on which to build. The model that grew out of the Latin American transitions, therefore, is, sadly, not applicable to Sub-Saharan Africa.

In recent years events in Sub-Saharan Africa have produced both hope and despair, often simultaneously. The early sixties were a time of hope and optimism for these new nations, followed in the later sixties and seventies by a huge wave of corrupt authoritarian governments. For a time in the 1980s it was thought, or hoped, that Africa would follow Latin America in transitioning to democracy, but those hopes were dashed, too. In the early nineties African economies were growing at only two percent a year—in other words, going backward as compared to population increases—but by the late nineties the earlier figure had doubled. The Clinton administration seized upon that growth and some limited democratization to proclaim an "African renaissance"; Assistant Secretary for African Affairs Susan Rice indicated optimistically that in countries "across the continent" legislators were being trained, independent judiciaries fostered, and cooperative work with churches, universities, and newspapers increased so as to build a strong civil society.[5]

But in recent years these optimistic projections have again been unrealized: war in the Congo enmeshing all its neighbors, new or renewed dictatorships, AIDS, economic downturn, greater joblessness, lowered life expectancy. Africa faces a bleaker future than at anytime in the past, according to a U.S. National Intelligence Estimate for the area; Sub-Saharan Africa is backsliding on every front. Stephen Morrison, the director of African Studies at the Washington–based Center for Strategic and International Studies (CSIS), says, "The number of simultaneous, multiple crises that the continent faces right now is unprecedented." He goes on, "Africa is in worse condition than ever before. And it's only going to get worse over the next generation." Chimes in Pauline Baker, an Africa expert and director of the Fund for Peace, "Even if you hold a free election in a collapsed state and elect a saint like Nelson Mandela, he'll be doomed to failure if there's no government structure." Particularly apropos this discussion of civil society, Baker concludes, "One man alone can't rule without institutions, many of which have eroded since independence."[6]

One needs, of course, to distinguish carefully between countries to appreciate the differences between them and the hopeful signs that still exist in some places, but that would require a far more detailed analysis than is possible here. A few illustrations, however, serve to indicate the variety of situations that exist and where civil society is sufficiently strong to hold out hope for the future. For example, the four most democratic governments in West Africa today—Benin, Ghana, Mali, and Senegal—all have flourishing private talk-radio stations, and an independent communications system is one of the hallmarks of civil society. Ghana itself, previously under the dictatorship of the charismatic Jerry Rawling, has recently witnessed its first-ever peaceful transition from one elected civilian government to another. If one asks why Senegal has been more successful than others in combating HIV infection, the answer lies in large part in its (relatively) strong civil society and community-based institutions that have produced a web of home-grown self-help responses.[7]

In Zimbabwe, the Democratic Republic of the Congo, Kenya, Tanzania, and Rwanda, Christian missionaries and support groups, both Catholic and Protestant, have helped create some of the only civil society groups that exist—schools, hospitals, teacher training programs, social service and development agencies—but they are often beset by woefully inadequate funding, shortages of personnel, and the inability to organize these programs on a national basis. In addition, the chaos of the surrounding society, rising crime, civil and international war, genocide, mammoth corruption, and recently the often violent challenge of close-by fundamentalist Islamic groups (an alternative expression of "civil society," or its antithesis?) have made these groups' activities more dangerous and more precarious, in some cases to the extent of forcing the Christian groups to abandon their useful projects.[8]

Nigeria is an especially important test case. With 120 million people, it is Africa's most populous country and its second largest (after South Africa) economy. It is the world's sixth largest exporter of oil. Potentially it is one of the richest countries in Africa, but actually it is one of the poorest and rapidly *losing* ground. When President (and former general) Olusegun Obasanjo returned to power in 1999 through democratic elections, hopes were high both for democracy and for civil society in Nigeria. But the country is deeply torn by ethnic, tribal, and religious strife. Corruption and violent crime are omnipresent. Even with all that oil and a creative population, the economy is stagnant or shrinking. President Obasanjo, though elected democratically, has moved in authoritarian directions and is ominously making the familiar arguments that all authoritarians make: that in the absence of strong institutions and a strong civil society, strong-man rule is necessary. Many Nigerians as well as international advisers fear that Sub-Saharan Africa's biggest and potentially richest country is fragmenting, falling apart. Civil society (what is left of it) seems on the verge of disintegrating.[9]

Nigeria is Africa's second largest economy, but what is the situation in the continent's largest economy, South Africa? Especially with the end of apartheid and the election of Nelson Mandela in 1994, South Africa seemed to have turned a corner. But since then South Africa has disappeared from the headlines and received little international attention. The world tends to assume that, as apartheid ended, South Africa's problems would also end. But as we see below, that has not occurred. Crime, violence, corruption, civil conflict, AIDS—all the problems associated with the rest of the continent—now afflict South Africa, too. Political fragmentation is also occurring there and civil society in both the black and white communities, many will be surprised to hear, is disintegrating. Let us proceed to the more detailed South Africa case study now.

SOUTH AFRICA

South Africa, where the primary first-hand research for this report was carried out, was supposed to be the exception to the general—and generally discouraging—pattern in Sub-Saharan Africa. First, under apartheid South Africa had been the last bastion in the world of legal, constitutional discrimination, and its destruction lent moral authority and purpose to the building of democracy and civil society there. Second, South Africa, with a per-capita income of $3,160 per year, is considerably richer than virtually all other countries in the area, is considered a "middle-income" country by the World Bank, and is *ten times* wealthier on a per-person basis than most of its neighbors and as "close" as one-tenth (as compared with one-hundredth for the others—about the level of Botswana or Panama but considerably below Argentina, Brazil, Chile, Mexico, or Venezuela) of the level of the world's wealthier countries.

Third, South Africa has a quite well-developed infrastructure not only of industry and commerce but also of institutions and civil society; its total gross national product marks it as the only industrialized country in Africa. Fourth, in 1994 South Africa had, for the first time, a truly democratic election that brought the heroic Nelson Mandela to power and seemed to offer hope for the country's overall prospects and the future of democracy there. Mandela's charisma, grace, and moderation helped bring the ruling African National Congress (ANC), formerly Marxist, back toward the center, and also made it harder for his successors to depart from the democratic course that he set. And fifth, South Africa became for a time the darling of the international community, a recipient of major foreign aid and advice (wanted or unwanted) and *the* locus of a great deal of generous, foreign-sponsored and -influenced nongovernmental organization (NGO) and civil society activity in Southern Africa. The sense was widespread, although usually unspoken, that if South Africa, given its wealth, resources, and advantages, could not establish democracy and a functioning civil society, no African state could. South Africa was thus not only important in its own right but also as a hoped-for model and test case for other African states.

South Africa has vast mineral resources, well-developed industry, diverse and productive agriculture, and an overall standard of living higher than most of its neighbors. But within this generally favorable picture there are vast problems. First, wealth is terribly unevenly distributed with the top 5–10 percent of the population enjoying an overwhelming preponderance of the wealth. Second, unemployment is high at 35–40 percent; another 25–30 percent may be underemployed, the total reaching 70 percent of the population. Third, the distribution of wealth and income follows clear racial lines, with most of the wealth, land, mines, and industry in the hands of the white population and most of the poverty and unemployment concentrated among the black population. Fourth, there is a disconnect between where political power is concentrated in the country and the holders of economic power: blacks now control the political structure and government through the African National Congress and its affiliated organizations/subsidiaries whereas whites are still overwhelmingly dominant in the economy. Fifth, racism is still a powerful force: most whites in the business, intellectual, and university-educated communities have accepted the post-apartheid changes and want the present black-controlled regime to succeed (they have no other options), but many nonuniversity, working-class whites remain resentful of the changes and are particularly hurt by the black regime's affirmative action programs that leave them out in the cold in terms of civil service, government, and even private employment—although few of these go so far as to advocate or act on the idea of toppling the ANC-controlled government. Meanwhile, many blacks remain resentful of white affluence and privilege, which helps explain spiraling crime and violence directed against whites, refuse to speak the Afrikaner language, which is associated with the old apartheid regime, and are at times motivated by efforts to gain revenge against whites.

Sixth, with the transfer of power to the ANC, black expectations were raised that they would immediately become better off; but that has not happened; frustration is, therefore, rising among the black population; and there are well-founded fears both of white recalcitrance to refuse to share the wealth more equitably and of blacks taking the law into their own hands and seizing white property violently as in neighboring Zimbabwe. Tensions are thus rising along class and racial lines; meanwhile, the political, social, economic, and institutional infrastructure of the country shows signs of decay and the potential for future breakdown.[10] We return to this point later in the discussion.

Elements of Political Culture

South Africa was settled and colonized mainly by the Dutch in the seventeenth century. There they found a diverse, scattered, indigenous population numbering in the millions. As with the British and French in North America, the Spanish and Portuguese in Latin America, and the French, Belgians, Germans, and British elsewhere in Africa, the Dutch carried with them to their colonies the language, institutions, and values of their home country of that particular time. And as with these other colonies, too, once established, these values and institutions gradually became locked in place and continued to reflect the time period of the initial discovery and settlement. Over time, colonies and mother countries evolved along different paths, with the colonies often representing "fragments" of the mother countries set down in new places and circumstances, adapting to local conditions, and gradually distancing themselves from or losing track of the main currents of European civilization—even while trying desperately from these distant places to stay in touch with their roots.[11]

The Dutch in South Africa were shaped powerfully by their Calvinist and entrepreneurial heritage. In part, that belief system was used to justify a two-class society and the separation of the races. Equally important was the South African Dutch Calvinists' identification with the Old Testament, the story of a people, like themselves, set down in a wilderness, isolated and alone, a people of God, outnumbered by huge ratios, facing severe dangers and hardships, with enemies all around, quasi-paranoid, and heroically struggling and surviving against the odds. It is within this biblical conception, this "siege mentality," that the later system of apartheid was born.[12] Black, "colored," English, Indian, and Moslem South Africans would, of course, see the issue quite differently.

While the Dutch gradually moved into the interior to clear fields, develop farming, and worship God in their own tradition, urban and coastal areas were gradually colonized and taken over by the British. Indian and Islamic settlers added to the diversity of the population. In the Boer War at the end of the nineteenth century, the Dutch and the

British fought each other for control of the colony, with the Dutch, defeated, "trekking" or moving even farther into the interior (whence the famous song came, "We Are Marching to Praetoria") and developing an even more advanced case of paranoia as God's people, now isolated and alone, under siege, and abandoned eventually even by their own home government in The Netherlands. Recall also how different their situation was from whites in America: in the United States, whites outnumbered blacks by about ten-to-one, which made it relatively easy to contemplate racial integration, whereas in South Africa the ratios were exactly reversed: 90 percent black and colored and about 10 percent white, which meant that full racial integration and the enfranchisement of blacks would *automatically*, *immediately*, and *permanently* mean the loss of power for whites.

It was these numbers that were so critical, as much as white racial attitudes, in explaining the apartheid system of racial separation. The whites, both Dutch and British, thought of themselves as representatives of a superior civilization. They created a top-down, corporatist, or "pillared" society that favored whites over blacks, meanwhile locking the social structure in place and preventing change. Afrikaner "civil society" aimed to establish a separate, corporatist, political community controlling all areas of social life. They thought of the blacks as animist, primitive, backward, and pagan, people whom they, missionary-style, would educate, Christianize, "civilize" in European ways, and assimilate. Although there was cruelty in the dominance of blacks by whites, white attitudes were generally more patronizing than hateful. Blacks were viewed as "children" who would have to be converted, trained, and assimilated into Christianity and Westernness. Given the numbers of blacks and their low level of education, this process would require generations, maybe centuries, not just years. But this process came to be seen as much too slow for the black population. In addition, it was assumed, in South Africa as elsewhere, that white, Western, European civilization was superior, more advanced, and had to lead and educate others; this was not a situation of equality and cultural relativism. And, given the numbers and the siege mentality of the white population, once blacks began mobilizing and demanding their rights, the response was a hardening of the shell of enforced racial separation into the apartheid system—although within both the Dutch and the British communities this was not by any means a unanimous view. Many whites, including in the Dutch Calvinist churches, came to favor a more liberal, integrated community.

The result in South Africa was the absence of a single, national, political culture. Instead, political culture was divided, organized around class, racial, and ethnic lines. There was an upper-class political culture and a lower-class political culture, and eventually a middle-class one. There was a white political culture and a black, African political culture. But within these categories there were further divisions. Among white groups were Dutch, British, Jewish, European immigrants of various nationalities and political cultures; within each of these were further distinctions based on politics, religion, ethnicity, ideology, identity, and a wide range of perspectives. Among blacks there was a rising political consciousness that would eventually lead to a successful challenge of the apartheid system, but within the black community, if that term could even be used, were wide differences depending on location, income, ideology, ethnicity, class, and social and political orientation. Nor should we forget the quite separate political cultures of the Indian, Islamic, colored (a mix of black and white), and other minority communities.[13]

South Africa was a mosaic, not a monolith; but it was also marked by the absence of a single, national political culture on which all could agree.

CIVIL SOCIETY AND STATE-SOCIETY RELATIONS

South Africa's system of civil society both reflects and reinforces the political-cultural foundations of which we have been speaking.[14] It also reflects racial, developmental, and socioeconomic differences within the society.

First, within white culture, civil society is not very much different from what it is in other Dutch, British, or European societies throughout the first world. There are clubs, churches, associations of many kinds, sports teams, and professional and business groups to which one belongs and/or gives allegiance. They provide a vast web of associability and a firm foundation for civil society. The trouble is that these groups were, for the most part, discriminatory and limited to the white population, and exclusionary toward blacks. In addition, since the end of apartheid and the growing fear and isolation of the white population, this kind of rich, thick, European-like civil society has gone into considerable decline. No longer having access to public funds that longtime control of the government provided has also hurt Afrikaner civil society.

There is (or was) also the more oppressive form of civil society associated specifically with apartheid and the long–dominant Afrikaner National Party (ANP). The Party had branches for everyone—youth, women, businessmen, etc.—who supported the party and who, like the parent organization, became more militant over the years. Such groups are not unusual in political parties and especially those with European roots; in addition, political parties and their ancillary organizations are generally considered a part of civil society, which we support. However, in the case of the National Party, as it faced increasing challenges including terrorism, a national liberation movement supported by the ANC and the South African Communist Party, and urban violence coming out of the black townships, it constructed a considerable web of secret, secretive, and often illegal counterterrorist groups, private militias, secret police units, and spy networks to counter the rising violence. Rather like skinheads, the Ku Klux Klan, or private militias in other societies, these groups were often called "fascist" and are not what we have in mind when we talk about civil society. Since the collapse of the apartheid regime, however, and the ouster of the ANP as the governing party, most of these groups and their activities have gone underground or else out of existence—although similar fringe groups are still out there operating in the private sector, perhaps even augmented as whites feel increasingly under siege.

In the black community, civil society is also facing severe problems. As militancy and opposition to the apartheid system increased in the 1980s, blacks organized a number of civic organizations—popularly known as "civics"—in the townships that played a key role in challenging and undermining the apartheid government. The civics were widely and favorably portrayed in the Western media, with the image being of "little David," armed only with stones and a smile, taking on the "Goliath" of the South African armed state. At the time it was thought that the civics, which were pictured benignly but were often the manipulated instruments of the ANC, the Communist Party, or terrorist groups, would form the basis for a vibrant, black, post-apartheid civil society.[15]

But it has not quite worked out that way. First, once the epic anti-apartheid struggle was won, black African civil society in general, no longer with a clear moral purpose, focus, or unambiguous goal, has atrophied, been marginalized, and gone into decline; there are now simply fewer, less enthused, less participatory groups, and with no special claim to moral authority, than during the great struggle of the early 1990s. Many civic groups that once seemed to hold great promise have either closed down or been forced to radically curtail their activities—precisely the opposite of what was supposed to happen once apartheid ended and democracy was established.

Second, among the civics specifically, there have been severe adjustment problems in going from "comrade" to "citizen"—that is, of adjusting to pluralism instead of a monolithic crusade, accommodation rather than confrontation, and democratic give-and-take rather than revolutionary street action. The civics movements were often trained in the ideology of Soviet and Third World Marxism and in the revolutionary, often violent tactics of Third World liberation movements; they have had a hard time abandoning these strategies and adjusting to the requirements of genuine liberalism and democracy.[16]

Third, since the end of apartheid, though there has been some flowering of civil society, there has also been tightened control by the ANC over its ancillary organizations: labor unions, youth groups, peasant groups, women's groups, and so on. Party and government have come closer together and almost merged into one. The ANC has sought to turn these civil society organizations into agencies of the ANC government, often at the cost of their autonomy and freedom. An independent and autonomous civil society now exists alongside an increasingly ANC- or state-dominated civil society.

Fourth and almost contradictorily, in the absence of much new investment and employment, some post-apartheid "civic" groups have been transformed into criminal gangs, drug or prostitution cartels, and even terrorist organizations that take the law on land reform or worker participation into their own hands. This has led both to an appalling increase in crime and violence and to an acceleration of "white flight," which means the wholesale, accelerating exodus of the professional, trained, intellectual, technical, entrepreneurial class whose departure South Africa cannot afford and which threatens potentially to turn the country into "just another" poor, miserable, African country.[17]

Fifth is the corporatism phenomenon: in some cases the black-controlled government has granted a virtual monopoly to certain favored black civic groups (sometimes called "associational socialism") so that they are able to dominate an entire sector of society. In other cases, such as with black farmers, the government has almost literally created a "civil society" group from scratch in order to fill a certain organizational space—or to prevent other groups, usually nongovernmental, from occupying it. In still others, which perhaps reflects the continuing Leninist orientation of some political leaders, the government has begun to use the fledgling civil society groups as top-down instruments of state control rather than as nascent grassroots organizations exercising influence from below. The government at times seems to favor not so much democratic, pluralist civil society but instead "democratic centralism," civil society of a particular or corporatist kind, that which supports the government or which it can control and co-opt.

Sixth and even more ominously, there is a considerable fear among objective observers in South Africa that the governing ANC, whose history has not always been democratic, may tire of the often cumbersome and time-consuming democratic process, declare a one-party state as in Zimbabwe, incorporate those groups favorable to itself as associated organizations under party hegemony, and move to undercut or destroy all independent civil society groups, keeping only those that are already branches of the ANC or that it can control by corporatist carrots and sticks. It is already using coercion and authoritarian measures to displace some groups and impose others in not very democratic fashion, or to blame some civil society groups—that is, the business community in this case—for neither fostering sufficient economic growth nor engendering black empowerment within the economy.

A neglected feature of the discussion of South African civil society is the degree to which it remains tribally dominated. Fully one-third of South Africa's blacks still live—even in this, the most modern and developed of African states—under tribal organization. Mostly rural, some of these ethnic groups live almost a completely separate and autonomous existence; others have been converted into "modern" political parties or interest groups independent of and often opposed to the ANC government. Chieftaincy is still the predominant way of choosing leaders within these groups.

Tribalism is usually identified with traditionalism and "backwardness." Some groups are largely self-governing, and the ANC government has tried by various means to get these tribal communities to adopt a secular, mayoral–town council form of government, which the ANC, of course, will certainly dominate. But so far that campaign has not been successful as many tribal entities prefer their own ways and leaders. At one level, tribalism may be considered traditional and unmodern, but at another it is also indigenous; and if we take seriously the notion that civil society, to be lasting, has to be built upon indigenous, home-grown roots, then in the African context—even South Africa—we must take tribalism seriously.[18]

The overall result of the overthrow of apartheid and the establishment of black-controlled government has thus not been the expected blossoming of civil society in the post-apartheid era but rather its atrophy, apathy, and even withering away. Now that the epic anti-apartheid battle is over, many former civil society members ask, what is the logic of continued involvement? Significantly, civil society's post-apartheid decline may be found in both the white and the black communities. And, increasingly, there is a trend toward greater corporatist civil society and perhaps a monolithic statist system, rather than away from it toward real, lasting pluralism and democratic civic involvement. Moreover, the civil society that continues to exist outside the state is increasingly divided and fragmented, and may not be very representative. Violence and intimidation are increasing, not decreasing; separatism of white, black, and colored communities remains a fact of life. Observers are agreed that there are many dangers lurking and not a happy situation of democratic, Tocquevillian associational life. Some scholars have gone so far as to say there is as yet no genuinely South African civil society, and that to the extent civil society there continues to reflect sharp ethnic lines, it is not conducive to democratic politics.[19]

The International Context

While the anti-apartheid struggle was ongoing, many international civil society groups were involved in South Africa. These included religious groups, human rights organizations, black and African-American groups, official U.S. government organizations (the National Endowment for Democracy—NED; the U.S. Institute of Peace—USIP, etc.), and many others. There was a cause to support; the cause seemed righteous; and a multivariegated American and international civil society plunged into the task.

But since then a number of things have happened. The "cause" has been accomplished; apartheid has been eliminated; and majority rule was established. International interest in South Africa has, therefore, subsided and so have the activities of the civil society groups earlier involved. The withdrawal of the outside funding, technical support, and personnel is, in fact, one of the key reasons for the decline and destabilization of the South African NGO community and of civil society in general. Many South African civil society groups now must make it on their own; the large number of those that have fallen by the wayside reflects the fact that they may have been in large measure creations of the international community to begin with and lack a strong indigenous base. Meanwhile, large numbers of persons who once formed the backbone of civil society have abandoned that sector and taken more lucrative, often patronage-based jobs in the government and civil service.

In addition, once apartheid was abolished and democracy established, foreign assistance shifted away from supporting civil society and toward economic development and good governance projects. And with the euphoria of victory in the anti-apartheid struggle now giving way to the sober realities of hard political and economic choices, quite a number of civil society groups are being used as scapegoats, blamed by the government either for the lack of progress or—in the case of AIDS or declining business investment—for failure to conform to government policy. At the same time the government's attitude toward AIDS—seeing it as a Western plot and failing to acknowledge the medical science that goes into its detection and cures—has discredited it in the eyes of much of the international NGO community. In turn, the decline in aid and attention from the international community demonstrates how fickle and unreliable that community can be, while the decline in so many areas of South African civil society shows how weak civil society remains.

Conclusion

As political scientists Hennie Kotze and Pierre Du Toit conclude from their survey research, South Africa is not now a "happy" or liberal democracy based on a strong civil society.[20] After all, illiberal and inegalitarian forms have a deep heritage in South Africa in both the black and the white communities, and there is a strikingly low level of political tolerance. Instead, they find a weak and divided civil society and a regime uncertain what to do about it or even its own future direction. The society has become increasingly polarized rather than consensual and peaceful. They find a multiply divided society, one that is Balkanized and violent, plagued by financial and organizational problems, with civil society serving as antagonists in a divided country, a government that has had and is having a hard time adjusting to pluralism, civic bodies that are strongly associated with partisan political groups that engage one another in conflicts that are highly uncivil, a fundamentally polarized society, and one that runs the risk of being torn apart at the seams. Moreover, persistent ethnic conflict and tension serve to undermine existing civil society further and prevent the emergence of new groups. They agree that a genuine civil society (liberal, pluralist, autonomous, democratic) has yet to be built in South Africa and that, until that is done, both state and regime in South Africa will remain undemocratic. Clearly in the South Africa case, the most-developed country in Africa, the cliché that civil society is not a panacea rings true; indeed, the situation is by now far worse than that and actually quite desperate.

None of this was supposed to happen, and it may come as a shock to those who believed that once the apartheid regime fell and blacks were in power, democracy and civil society would certainly flower. But, in fact, tensions are as high now as ever and South Africa could rather easily degenerate into violence, a one-party state, and/or civil war. The withdrawal of so many of the international NGOs once the overriding goal—black power—had been achieved and the fact that they were no longer paying such close attention to the country help explain why they are now shocked to discover how tense and deteriorating the situation is. Racial tension and confrontations are again rising; public services are breaking down; the economy is deteriorating; crime and corruption are rampant; unemployment and violence are increasing; investment has slowed significantly; and both capital and whites are fleeing.[21] Both democracy and civil society are under siege.

If we now move, as a final comment, back to the other, far less-developed countries of Africa, we find an at least equally interesting, but if anything even less hopeful, situation of civil society. First, we find a number of civil society groups that are largely the reflection of

American or Western foreign aid agencies, that lack indigenous roots, that are often created specifically for the purpose of looking good to the foreign donors and attracting their money, but that have no prospects or intentions of blossoming into genuinely home-grown, grassroots, democratic organizations. Second, we have a large number of religious or historically missionary or church-connected civil society groups that *are* often democracy and development oriented but that are extremely fragile, underfunded, and often under attack by state authorities or Islamic fundamentalists.[22] Third, we have government-created or corporatist civil society groups that are often similarly in it for the money, to serve as props of authoritarian regimes, or to give the appearance of democracy without affording it real substance. Finally, we have genuine and indigenous civil society groups, often in the form of ethnic or tribal organizations, that *do* provide a measure of social services, socialization, police and judicial protection, etc., but that are often denounced as "primitive" or "traditional" and frequently undermined both by their own governments and by international aid donors and civil society groups. The situation of civil society in Sub-Saharan Africa is not healthy, and it may be getting worse rather than better.[23]

My overall conclusion agrees with that of Stephen Orvis. I believe that in Sub-Saharan Africa civil society has been defined too narrowly, largely to echo Western concepts; at the same time, too much (a new basis for democracy and development) has been asked of it. An accurate portrayal of Sub-Saharan African civil society would have to include patron-client relations, traditional authorities (chiefs, others), ethnic or tribal organizations, and maybe even criminal groups and rival militias or fighting forces. It is clear that not all of these groups or agencies are democratic. On the other hand, they *do* constitute elements of a Sub-Saharan system of civil society. We may, therefore, conclude, as does Orvis, that civil society has a stronger basis in Sub-Saharan Africa than we have often thought; on the other hand, it may not serve as the basis for peaceful, pluralist democracy that we might wish.[24]

64   4: SUB-SAHARAN AFRICA

NOTES

1. For the general background see Basil Davidson, *The Black Man's Burden: Africa and the Curse of the Nation State* (New York: New York Times Books, 1992); Ali A. Mazrui, *The Africans: A Triple Heritage* (London: BBC Publications, 1986); Naomi Chazan et al., *Politics and Society in Contemporary Africa* (Boulder: Lynne Rienner, 1992); John W. Harbeson et al., *Civil Society and the State in Africa* (Boulder: Lynne Rienner, 1994).

2. *South Africa: A Country Study* (Washington, D.C.: U.S. Government Printing Office, 1981); Crawford Young, *The African Colonial State in Comparative Perspective* (New Haven: Yale University Press, 1994); Michael Bratton and Nicolas van de Welle, *Democratic Experiments in Africa: Regime Transitions in Comparative Perspective* (Cambridge: Cambridge University Press, 1997).

3. Jannie Gagiano and Pierre Du Toit, "Consolidating Democracy in South Africa: The Role of Civil Society," in Hennie Kotze (ed.), *Consolidating Democracy: What Role for Civil Society in South Africa* (Stellenbosch, South Africa: University of Stellenbosch Press, 1996), pp. 47–73.

4. Tracy Kuperus, "Building Democracy: An Examination of Religious Associations in South Africa and Zimbabwe," *Journal of Modern African Studies*, 37, 4 (1999), 643–668.

5. Geneva Overholser, "Africa's Growing Pains," *The Washington Post* (October 17, 1998), p. A21.

6. The quotes are from Robin Wright, "Africa Faces Crises, Bleak Future," *Los Angeles Times* (August 27, 2000).

7. Thomas L. Friedman, columns in *New York Times* (April 28 and May 2, 2001).

8. Kuperus, "Building Democracy."

9. "Nigeria," *Financial Times Survey* (April 9, 2002).

10. Pierre Du Toit, *South Africa's Brittle Peace: The Problem of Post-Settlement Violence* (London: MacMillan, 2001).

11. Louis Hartz (ed.), *The Founding of New Societies* (New York: Harcourt, Brace, Jovanovich, 1964).

12. T. Dunbar Moody, *The Rise of Afrikanerdom: Power, Apartheid, and the Afrikaner Civil Religion* (Berkeley: University of California Press, 1975).

13. Pierre Du Toit, *State-Building and Democracy in Southern Africa: Botswana, Zimbabwe, and South Africa* (Washington, D.C.: United States Institute of Peace Press, 1995).

14. Wilmot James and Daria Caliguire, "Renewing Civil Society," *Journal of Democracy*, 7 (January 1996), 56–66; Daryl Glaser, "South Africa and the Limits of Civil Society," *Journal of Southern African Studies*, 23 (March 1997), 5–25; more generally Marina Ottaway, *Africa's New Leaders: Democracy or State Reconstruction?* (Washington, D.C.: Carnegie Endowment, 1999).

15. Glenn Adler and Jonny Steinberg, *From Comrades to Citizens: The South African Civics Movement and the Transition to Democracy* (London: MacMillan, 2000).

16. Adler and Steinberg, *Comrades to Citizens.*

17. Du Toit, *Brittle Peace.*

18. Jon Jeter, "Tribal Ways vs. Modern Government: South Africa's Ruling Party in Conflict with Age-Old Tradition," *The Washington Post* (December 18, 2000), p. A1; also Pierre Du Toit and Jannie Gagiano, "Strongmen on the Cape Flats," *Africa Insight*, 23, 2 (1993), 102–111.

19. Hennie Kotze and Pierre Du Toit, "The State, Civil Society, and Democratic Transition in South Africa," *Journal of Conflict Resolution*, 39 (March 1995), 27–48.

20. Kotze and Du Toit, "The State."

21. Clarence Page, "After Apartheid," syndicated column, *New Bern* (N.C.) *Sun Journal* (July 19, 2000), p. A6.

22. Kuperus, "Building Democracy."

23. Richard Cornwell, "The Collapse of the African State," in Jakkie Cilliers and Peggy Mason (eds.), *Peace, Profit, or Plunder? The Privatization of Security in War-Torn African Societies* (Pretoria, South Africa: Institute for Security Studies, 1999), pp. 61–80.

24. Stephen Orvis, "Civil Society in Africa or African Civil Society?" *Journal of Asian and African Studies*, 36 (February 2001), 1–29.

5

EAST ASIA

East Asia has some of the world's most dynamic economies and societies. Japan has the second largest economy (after the United States) in the world and is among the world's most prosperous countries with a high standard of living. South Korea, Hong Kong, Singapore, and Taiwan have also experienced miracle economic growth over the last four decades, beginning in the 1960s as still Third World countries but then *leapfrogging* over other countries (relatively rare in the rank ordering of the wealth of nations, which has stayed quite constant over the last hundred years) to take their place among what the World Bank calls high-income countries. Although somewhat less dramatically and impressively, Malaysia, Thailand, the Philippines, Indonesia, and now China, Vietnam, and Myanmar have also experienced impressive but irregular economic growth.

One would expect such vibrant economies to also have developed vibrant civil societies, and to some extent they have. But as compared to Western Europe or North America, especially relative to their level of socioeconomic development, East Asia for the most part still has weak civil society. "Strong states [in the sense of authoritative, bureaucratic, centralized decision making], weak societies" is the catch phrase that is generally employed to summarize the situation.[1] The question we wrestle with here is why East Asian civil society remains weak despite the area's impressive, even phenomenal, economic growth.

Socioeconomic Data

East Asia has some of the most developed, most expansive economies in the world. Table 5.1 provides some basic data on the region's economies, their levels of social modernization, and their rank ordering among the world's nations.

One would expect, from development theory, that countries with such high socioeconomic rankings would also have well-developed civil societies. Because these are countries—at least those at the top ranks—that have a sizable middle class, high literacy, high urbanization, low unemployment, low income inequalities, regular elections, and a functioning democracy. The theory of development, at least as articulated in the West and based on the Western model, leads us to expect that such countries will also have strong civil societies.

But that is not the case. In fact, East Asia has a notoriously weak civil society. Or, put in developmental terms, relative to its level of socioeconomic development, East Asia has a relatively weakly developed civil society.

Elements of Political Culture

East Asia, unlike the United States, has no history of civil society in the Tocquevillian or Madisonian sense, denoting webs of popular or grassroots associability. Most of the East Asian countries surveyed here are remarkably *civil*, in terms of absence of crime, absence of direct confrontation, and quiet, nonconflictual interpersonal relations; but civil society in the sense of vast networks of independent associations standing between the individual and the state and serving as a check on governmental authority is largely absent.[2]

Let us begin at the beginning, with language.[3] Most of Asia has no language equivalents for such key concepts as "public" (as in "public interest"), "civil," or even "society." The standard translation for public in Japan is *kç*, derived from a Chinese character (which, therefore, means it has approximately the same meaning throughout East Asia)

Table 5.1[a]   East Asian Indicators of Socioeconomic Development

Country	GNP	GNP per capita	Life expectancy		Literacy		Urban Percent	GNP per capita rank
			Male	Female	Male	Female		
Japan	4,078.9	32,230	77	84	100		79	6
Singapore	95.4	29,610	75	79	96	88	100	9
Hong Kong	161.7	23,520						20
South Korea	397.9	8,490	74	80	99	96	81	51
Taiwan	160.0	8,400	74	80	99	93	80	52
Malaysia	77.3	3.400	70	75	91	82	57	72
Thailand	121.0	1,960	46	48	83	64	21	102
Philippines	78.0	1,020	67	71	95	95	58	131
China	980.2	780	68	72	91	75	32	140
Indonesia	119.5	580	64	67	91	80	40	150
Myanmar		755 or lower[b]	58	62	89	79	27	
Vietnam (formerly Burma)	28.2	370	66	71	95	91	20	167
Cambodia	3.0	260	52	55	57	20	16	186

SOURCE: World Bank, *World Development Report 2000–2001.*

[a]Countries listed in declining order of per-capita income.

[b]Estimates by World Bank.

that suggests "government" or "ruling authority" more than it does "public." Most Japanese, when they hear the word *kɔ̃*, assume it means government or state, or more specifically state bureaucracy, not so much public or popular or grassroots organizations. The concept of "public" in the Western sense is still not very familiar in Japan. The obvious implication is that, for the Japanese and other East Asians, state interests tend to dominate over public interests, with largely negative consequences for civil society. We return to this theme shortly.

Much the same applies to "civil" and "society." The term "civil" in East Asia tends to refer to "proper," age-old, and accustomed interpersonal relations and Asian expectations of appropriate behavior, which are deferential, submissive, and hierarchically derived, not so much implying "civic" or popular participation in governmental affairs. Similarly with "society," for which there is no equivalent Japanese translation either.

Whereas *kÇ* is a concept implying vertical, hierarchical, and top-down (or state) relationships, "society," which suggests a horizontal and even spontaneous association of individuals, is also a foreign concept in the East Asian tradition. A wide variety of words and phrases were tried before *shakai* came to be commonly used as the standard rendering of "society." The absence of Japanese and, in general, East Asian equivalents for such terms as "public," "civil," and "society" is symbolic. Most Americans and, of course, all civil society advocates think of the modern democratic state as founded on a strong civil society base where the concept of "public" or "public interest" is indispensable. But in historically Confucian, top-down, hierarchical, authoritarian East Asia, such fundamental terms have either been absent historically or they carry different meanings than in the American or Western context.

The reasons these terms are absent or unfamiliar in East Asia is that democracy itself, and its necessary accompanying notions of grassroots or popular participation, has long been absent from the area and is a relatively new, and perhaps not yet deeply imbedded, concept. The tradition historically in East Asia is instead one of respect for authority and disdain for the masses. Neither in Confucian nor in Buddhist theory is there a concept of "the people" nor of "civil society" nor even of democracy. Instead the assumption at least in the past is of the overwhelming superiority of "the state," the state bureaucracy, or officialdom. Decisions were authoritatively, if not authoritarianly, made from the top down, not from the bottom up. The assumption was (and still is) that the government alone is best able to judge what is in the public interest. The Confucian concept is thus close to the Rousseauian tradition in the West, wherein the ruler knows the "general will," need not necessarily check with the public or electorate about his decisions, and civil society as the West knows it is neither present nor seen as desirable.[4]

In such a top-down context, any attempt to understand East Asia in the light of "civil society" is bound to be frustrating. Under the East Asian bureaucratic or authoritarian state, the government represents the *whole* and is *the* authority embodying the public, whereas the people are simply considered subordinate parts of that larger system, perhaps pursuing their private interests but even then under official or state authority. Until these deeply held cultural beliefs in the superiority of authority and disdain for the public are overcome, and until the belief is widespread that the people themselves are worthy of respect and have individual as well as group value, a strong civil society is unlikely to emerge.[5]

All of the East and Southeast Asian cultures have devolved elaborate rules for conducting interpersonal relationships, including between government and governed, but almost all of these are defined in hierarchical rather than egalitarian terms.[6] Formality and correctness are expected but not necessarily equality. Superior-inferior relationships are designed to glorify the dignity of the superior and to ensure that the inferior knows and stays in his/her place. Superiors are especially sensitive to real or perceived slights or challenges to their status. The political effect, therefore, is to reinforce authoritarian norms and retard the development of interest-group or civil society bargaining and give-and-take that are essential to democracy. This is changing, of course, as democracy has come to the area, but the *form* of democracy that is practiced still tends to be top-down, bureaucratic, and state-centric.

Instead of civil society in the Western sense, much of East and Southeast Asia is dominated by networking or patron-client ties of greater or lesser complexity. In Japan, interpersonal ties are based on the concepts of *ou* and *giri*, which entail a powerful sense of obligation, indebtedness, and reciprocity. The Chinese system is that of *quanxi*, or personal connections, which is a firmly structured, institutionalized arrangement for ensuring and perpetuating mutual obligation. Both Indonesia and the Philippines have elaborate systems of patron-client relations that reach all the way from local to national levels and back down again. Burma (now Myanmar) and Thailand also have patronage networks—in a sense these are the functional equivalents of civil society—but they are less elaborately structured and often involve little more than norms of civility, without elaborate networking and top-to-bottom patronage channels. Tribe, ethnicity, and regionalism are also components of civil society in Southeast Asia. The line between patronage and outright corruption is often obscure.

An examination of these East and Southeast Asian patron–client systems reveals a number of interesting conclusions. First, in contrast to the Western attitude that in such systems patrons have all the advantages and clients are always exploited, in Asia it is often the clients who *force* their patrons to take risks in order to gain more power and influence so that the clients may also benefit from the advantages gained. Second, there are few signs that this Asian system is giving way, as is the presumption in the West whether from liberal, Marxist, or bureaucratic perspectives, under the impact of modernization. Indeed, thirdly, many Asian figures—Lee Quan, Yew, Muhammed Mathitir—tout their model of a strong state and weak society as essential to Asian development, a model that is not only successful but reflects Asian values and indigenous traditions more closely than does the American system of civil society based on conflictual interest-group bargaining. Fourth, as Asian society does modernize and takes on the institutional accoutrements imported from the United States or the West, such as political parties, interest groups, and civil society, these so-called "modern" institutions remain heavily infused with some patron-client relations of the past, now updated and given Western dress.[7]

In much of Asia, whether in "communist" or "democratic" systems, it is still mainly the state and the state bureaucracy that govern, still in a top-down and authoritative rather than a grassroots, liberal, and popular/participatory way. The legitimation of group or individual interests separate from the state or community has been quite slow in coming and even now is not well established.[8] Private interests and individual personalities, apart from the group, firm, or government agency, are still viewed as shameful expressions of selfishness and greed.* Behind the glitter of the recent East Asian economic miracles, hence, is not so much a system of liberal, democratic capitalism and competition but an often more sordid system of special favoritism, bribery, and indistinct lines between public and private entrepreneurship.

---

*During my research in China, my guide, a graduate student in political science in Beijing who later came to the United States to study, told me that she was "working on developing my individual personality." Such a comment sounds strange to Western ears since we assume all of us since babyhood have individual personalities, but in China with its communalist tradition one has to *work* at developing such individualism.

Particularly relevant to our discussion here, America's foremost Asia specialist, Lucian Pye, argues that East and Southeast Asian societies are not deficient in norms of civility, social capital, or even some forms of civil society.[9] Rather, he says, they have been combined in ways that are very different from those of the West. Asian cultures, he argues, are particularistic, resistant to a universalist formula, or else *selectively* incorporate those institutions of the West that can best be adapted to Asian ways of doing things. For example, in Singapore, Malaysia, China, and other societies to a somewhat lesser degree, the "community" is identified with the state and state policy, so that any pressure from civil society in opposition to state policy is viewed as both an affront to the community and, dangerously, a subversive activity inviting retribution. In the most developed countries—Japan, Singapore, Hong Kong, Taiwan, South Korea—what passes for "civil society" is so intertwined with government/bureaucratic/administrative agencies and state decision making as to be all but inseparable from them. Throughout Asia, what we call state-society relations or civil society is played out at a much lower level than American or European interest-group theory would suggest, at the level of the family, the clan, the neighborhood, and the immediate, face-to-face community. So that even when the figures show a quantum increase in recent years in civil society groups in Japan and other countries, that does not mean necessarily an increase in American-style pluralism, interest-group competition, or grassroots democracy. But that also means that there is still a *huge* space between these lower-level, often local or neighborhood associations and the state, with relatively little civil society in between. And that absence of strong intermediary associations makes both democracy and stability in much of the region quite tenuous.

STRUCTURAL CHANGE AND ASIAN STATE-SOCIETY RELATIONS

As long as Asia remained relatively underdeveloped, traditionalist (Confucianist), and plagued by both internal (disorder) and external (Cold

War) issues, it was relatively easy to maintain a closed, top-down, state-centric, bureaucratic-authoritarian political system. But as Asian society modernized, as globalization had its cultural and social effects, and then as the Cold War ended, new openings, new space for civil society, began to emerge. Peter Moody calls this new era in Asia "post-Confucian."[10]

Japan, South Korea, and Taiwan—along with Singapore, the most developed countries in Asia—are the primary cases. In all three, à la W. W. Rostow, the patterns were similar—and, of course, South Korea and Taiwan had the earlier Japanese model to look to. In all three, economic development was initially, and for a considerable period, given priority over political development, or democratization. That is, in all three countries it was seen as necessary first to stimulate economic growth and to establish the conditions for economic growth—order, stability, a climate favorable to investment and export-led growth—before the "dangerous" pluralism and freedom of democracy could be permitted. That meant strong, centralized decision making, a powerful and effective state-bureaucratic structure, concentrated economic power, close interconnections between business and the state, as well as strict controls and limits (of a quasi-corporatist kind) on human rights, freedom of association, speech, assembly, pluralism, and especially student and labor union activity. Only after stability had been achieved, a strong economy developed, a sizable middle class had emerged, and the internal and external threats ended could genuine freedom and pluralism be permitted.

And that is generally the pattern followed. Japan led the way with export-led economic growth beginning in the 1950s and 1960s, achieved "miracle" growth rates in the 1960s and 1970s, and emerged by the 1980s as the second most powerful economy in the world (after only the United States) and with one of the world's highest standards of living. South Korea and Taiwan followed (also Hong Kong and Singapore, but they are essentially city-states with special circumstances and thus somewhat distinct cases), utilizing the Japanese model and perhaps applying it even more strictly than did Japan: strong, even authoritarian government, centralized decision making, close collaboration between the bureaucratic state and the entrepreneurial sector, and tight control on freedom and group activity. By the late 1960s Japan was called the economic "tiger" of Asia; by the late 1970s the other four were referred to as the "little tigers." Their economic growth rates were not only spectacular but also virtually unprecedented in world history, vaulting them over other countries, from poverty to affluence, from Third World to First World.

Democratization, however, lagged behind. Japan had a democratic constitution and had been occupied and was closely monitored by the United States so that authoritarianism and human rights abuses were limited; but it remained essentially a one-party state that limited civil liberties, maintained strict order and uniformity, and kept close control over pluralist group activities. South Korea and Taiwan, both flash points in the Cold War, maintained authoritarian or "bureaucratic-authoritarian," one-party systems, where the army was either in power or so close to the surface of power as to be inseparable from it, and employed repressive controls and violence against student, labor, and opposition groups.[11] The Philippines (Ferdinand Marcos) and Indonesia (Raden Suharto) maintained military-authoritarian regimes that for a long time paid not even lip service to democracy. Singapore was an especially interesting case (and an exception to the general pattern) in that it maintained authoritarian controls and restrictions on civil liberties even *after* economic growth had been achieved, a strong middle class had emerged, and the internal (potential for ethnic conflict, civil, gang warfare) and external threats had largely disappeared.

It was only in the 1980s and 1990s, after the security issues had been mainly settled, significant development had been achieved, a middle class consolidated, and a consensus established on future social and political directions, that South Korea and Taiwan—both following somewhat separate routes—determined they could move toward greater pluralism and political democracy. Greater press freedom was allowed; opposition political parties were permitted that eventually even won elections; and, especially important for this study's purposes, greater freedom of association, assembly, and group activity was, somewhat grudgingly, authorized. In other words, it was only *after* significant economic growth had been achieved and social and political stability established that South Korea and Taiwan concluded they could afford the *luxury* of genuinely free, pluralist, and competitive civil society.[12]

But all this was achieved only with great anguish, reluctance on the part of government authorities, and struggle on the part of opposition groups. It was by no means automatic, according to some universal or global model of change, nor so antiseptic as presented in the preceding paragraph. Rather, it was the result of struggle and constant pressure on the part of student, labor, and other opposition groups, clash and contradiction between them and governing authorities, and sometimes violence and bloodshed. "Civil society" is not something, like Athena emerging fully formed from the head of Zeus, that springs up automatically, spontaneously, universally, or through the good offices and best intentions of civil society advocates; rather, it is the result of struggle, pressure, clash, and conflict.

The first issue, for our purposes, was the language problem: how to find a terminology for "civil society," "pluralism," and even "public interest" that overcame the absence of such ideas and concepts in historic Asian thought. This is essentially a problem of finding new meaning in old terms and is thus a problem of political culture. We have said that in traditional Japanese and in other Asian languages, there are no real equivalents to these key terms; and even when linguists, societal actors, and politicians began to search for such equivalents as, for example, in the Japanese term *kＣeki* for "public interest," the emphasis was still overwhelmingly on the official or government or state-centered interpretation of this term rather than the societal or "public." But gradually over the last twenty years, we have witnessed a wrestling with this issue and an evolution of language to accommodate these new understandings—even while actual official and even popular usage still lags behind, putting emphasis even now on the state or top-down side more than on the bottom-up or civil society side.[13]

A second issue was the use of public interest issues in Japan and East Asia more generally during the 1980s and 1990s that mobilized citizens' participation and led to a quite dramatic rise in civil society activism. Quite a number of these new movements arose in response to, or as a result of, large-scale economic, social, and political transformations that had occurred over the preceding thirty years and were still unfolding. The most significant of these were the democracy and people's movements in South Korea, Taiwan, the Philippines, and later Indonesia as well, although in the latter country what might be termed "premature democratization" seemed to be producing fragmentation and possibly national disintegration and ungovernability rather than happy, democratic, civil society. These movements pushed for genuine democracy, real opposition political parties that would have a chance at winning, and more "Western" or at least updated conceptions of human rights, including not just the classic freedoms but also individual rights as well as the historic group rights.

In Japan, which had had regular elections for some time and was at least a formal democracy, the changes were less dramatic in terms of capturing headlines but perhaps equally significant in long-range terms. There, the mobilization of a historically deferential (to the state as well as to superiors) people around such issues as opposition to the building of a new airport outside Tokyo, environmental and pollution controls on major industries, park projects in large cities that were built without consulting the residents, and rescue and relief projects in Kobe after the 1995 earthquake showed that private nongovernmental organizations (NGOs) and nonprofit organizations (NPOs) were far quicker and more effective at responding to popular needs than governmental agencies, and led to a major proliferation of civil society groups throughout Japan.[14]

In Japan, and to a somewhat lesser extent in the other countries, there has been a veritable groundswell in the growth of civil society. The rise of "public" consciousness on a variety of issues has gone hand in hand with greater citizens' activism and, hence, in the growth of civil society. As of 1996, over 85,000 groups were registered as NGOs or NPOs, involved in a wide range of activities from welfare and education to human rights, peace, the environment, even garbage collection. In the realm of international cooperation, Japan had only seven groups registered at the end of the 1960s, thirty-three at the end of the 1970s, one hundred thirty-two at the end of the 1980s, and over two hundred by the turn of the millennium. Volunteerism, another mark of an emerging civil society, is also up significantly: 1.3 million people were mobilized to assist with relief activities after the Kobe earthquake and 270,000 workers were mobilized to save coastal areas when a Russian tanker carrying crude oil ran ashore on the Japanese coast in 1997. There has been, in other words, a tremendous growth in the last twenty years in Asian democratic groups, people's movements, and civil society.[15] But remember how many of these are still only temporary, organized only at the local level, and are not really national interest groups or civil society in the American sense.

While this growth, even with the qualifications noted, is encouraging to civil society advocates, the situation in East and Southeast Asia is still far from the unfettered interest-group pluralism, diversity, and competition of U.S. or European democracy. Rather, the system is still one of predominantly state-structured interest-group activity, or corporatism, combined with some elements of free associability as well, as sometimes informal, sometimes violent street action. In Japan, for example, the concept of "public interest corporation" now exists in the law and civil code, but confirmation of an organization's "public interest" orientation by central government authorities is still the condition for authorization of its legal status. The power to grant such legal status, however, is also the power to deny or delay it, thus depriving the group of all-important legitimacy before the law. Moreover, even after incorporation, these groups remain under the guidance and supervision of the state and its ministries; there is no automatic human right of free associability. Furthermore, of the 26,000 public interest corporations registered in Japan, a sizable percentage are aimed at providing post-retirement employment for the country's legion career civil servants, thus reinforcing once again the old public-equals-official structure. Civil society has clearly grown in Japan but there is less there than meets the eye, and much of what does exist is still controlled, regulated, or absorbed into the state in corporatist, not necessarily liberal, fashion.

Japan is, of course, the most developed of the Asian countries, and perhaps the most "democratic," which may or may not be saying a lot. In countries that are less developed than Japan, and where civil society is less advanced, the balance may still be powerfully on the side of the state and less so on the side of civil society. For example, while South Korea and Taiwan have both taken some enormous strides toward democracy in the last decade, that process is still incomplete; civil society is still weak and often tenuous; and such fundamental pluralist groups as students, labor, and political parties may still be subject to government harassment, controls, regulation, and conceivably even, in the worst of circumstances, elimination. Proceeding farther south to the Philippines, Indonesia, and Southeast Asia, the situation of civil society may be even more perilous because the state or the army not only possesses great power but also the ability literally to dissolve, repress, and eliminate civil society. In addition, in countries such as Indonesia and several of the others mentioned, "civil society" often means tribal, local, ethnic, or regional power; and the devolution of decision making to these groups may result in the breaking up or disintegration of the *national* political system. Not only is civil society thus often perilous or on shaky grounds throughout the region, but also there is a fairly close correlation between development and the health of civil society, with Japan (even with all its limits) on the top, followed by South Korea and Taiwan, and other countries with considerably weaker societies. And even there, as Shin'icki Yoshida has written, the entire political process represents even now a competition between the public-equals-official society and the forces for freedom from the fetters of that society.[16]

THE INTERNATIONAL CONTEXT

The more developed nations in East Asia—Japan, now South Korea, Taiwan, and Singapore—have *not* been the subject of major focus by international civil society groups. These countries have not been in the headlines recently as major democracy or human rights violators; moreover, they are often viewed by the international NGO/civil society community as being sufficiently developed economically and successful politically that they have "graduated" from the list of countries to aid or even to be concerned about.

Within these countries, furthermore, the focus of concern is often not so much the encouragement of more civil society per se or as a bulwark of liberal democracy in the American mode, but rather how to create civil society organizations that will make them *look* more acceptable to the international community or, in the case of often isolated Taiwan, that will assist in their forging international connections that will bolster their foreign policy, which is frequently hampered by the Mainland's (People's Republic of China) insistence that Taiwan be isolated and not aided by *any* international group. In both Japan and South Korea civil society groups are often created by the state as a way of making them look good to the outside world or to Westerners—the "imitation of the West" effect. In Taiwan, NGOs are strongly encouraged not for their own sake but as a way of improving the appearance of Taiwanese democracy, which is seen as its primary diplomatic resource, and as a way, through their international activities, of enhancing the island's diplomatic presence abroad and breaking out of its international isolation. Since Taiwan's official representation in other countries and international agencies is often limited by Beijing's refusal to allow it, Taiwan's usually quasi-official NGOs provide an alternative channel.[17] But this is, of course, far from what most advocates of civil society have in mind.

When we get to the less-developed areas of Asia—the Philippines, Indonesia, Southeast Asia—even more serious problems emerge. In the Philippines, while there was a massive mobilization of civil society in the mid-1980s, first against the dictatorship of Ferdinand Marcos and then *for* the "people's movement" election of Corey Aquino, after that crisis-of-the-moment civil society went into decline. Civil society was mobilized again in opposition to later President Joseph Estrada, but one could arguably make the case that that was as much *destructive* of democracy, stability, and national unity as it was an expression of some degree of popular will. In Indonesia, civil society was encouraged by Western agencies as a way of undermining the dictatorship of Radin Suharto and encouraging democracy; but with the decline and possible disintegration of Indonesia, in part because of this effort, into strife, fragmentation, religious conflict, and separatism, one would be hard pressed to say that it is a shining example of successful civil society accomplishment. Finally, in Southeast Asia (Cambodia, Laos, Myanmar, Thailand, Vietnam), where the international community has made a substantial effort to support civil society, relatively little democratization or development has as yet resulted.

The situation in the two key, transitional countries of Indonesia and the Philippines is especially complex. First, in both countries there has been in recent years, associated with the transitions to democracy, a proliferation of new civil society groups dedicated to such causes as human rights, greater freedom, the environment, honesty in government, the advancement of women, judicial reform, and democratization. Second and at the same time, the government has moved, corporatist style, to co-opt these groups or to create parallel organizations that it can more easily control. Third and again simultaneously, there are a variety of new public-private partnerships, what are sometimes called (contradictorily) governmental-nongovernmental organizations (GNGOs), that represent efforts to bridge the gap between the historic statism of these countries and the rise of a more dynamic private sector. Finally and again simultaneously, we have the problem that to the extent civil society comes to focus on such issues as Islamic fundamentalism or the aspirations of separatist movements in Mindanao (the Philippines) or Aceh (Indonesia), it may contribute to nondemocratic outcomes in the first instance or the disintegration of the central state itself in the second.

CONCLUSION

A number of conclusions stand out from this analysis:

1. With their strong Confucian and non-Western traditions, many Asian societies have had a hard time conceiving of civil society or even finding the proper words to describe it.

2. When they do, they tend to think of public, group, and state actions as distinct from the Western conception of private, individual, and grassroots activities.

3. This orientation leads often to state-centered and state-controlled (or corporatist) systems of civil society.

4. Nevertheless, civil society and associational life have flourished in Japan, South Korea, and Taiwan, recently in Indonesia and the Philippines (less so in other countries), mainly around local environmental and other less overtly political issues—that is, issues that are "safe" and do not challenge the state in its essentials.

5. There remains a strong emphasis on creating civil society, not for its own sake but in order to imitate and look good to outside observers.

6. The growth of civil society is correlated closely with socioeconomic development, especially in South Korea and Taiwan. As development occurred, ruling elites felt they could allow greater space for civil society. But that is still within the limits of predominantly statist systems.

7. Civil society is often associated with crises or transitions, such as post-authoritarian transitions to democracy; once the crisis is over, civil society tends to decline.

8. Civil society has not been an unmitigated success: it can lead to instability as in the Philippines or to fragmentation and possible disintegration as in Indonesia.

9. Even in the present era of rapid change and democratization, civil society in Asia remains weak, underdeveloped, and centered mainly on local or nonthreatening (to the state) issues. Meanwhile, state, bureaucratic, and private/public administrative agencies remain overwhelmingly dominant.

10. The growth of civil society is not inevitable or unilinear; under the threat of war, terrorism, ethnic strife, political instability, or Islamic fundamentalism, some hitherto increasingly democratic states (e.g., Singapore) may decide to restrict civil society activities.

11. The situation in many countries represents a mix of new, more democratic civil society, statist or corporatist tendencies, new

public-private partnerships, civil society that is not necessarily democratic, and separatist movements that may lead to national disintegration.

NOTES

1. For background, see W. T. DeBary, *Asian Values and Human Rights: A Confucian Communitarian Perspective* (Cambridge: Harvard University Press, 1998); Gerald Curtis, *The Logic of Japanese Politics: Leaders, Institutions, and the Limits of Change* (New York: Columbia University Press, 1999); Peter Moody, *Political Opposition in Post-Confucian Society* (New York: Praeger, 1988); also Lionel Jensen, *Manufacturing Confucianism: Chinese Traditions and Universal Civilization* (Durham, N.C.: Duke University Press, 1997).

2. The best source is Yamamoto Tadashi (ed.), *Deciding the Public Good: Governance and Civil Society in Japan* (Tokyo: Japan Center for Educational Exchange, 1999).

3. Shin'icki Yoshida, "Rethinking the Public Interest in Japan: Civil Society in the Making," in Tadashi (ed.), *Deciding*, pp. 13–50.

4. Peter Moody, *Tradition and Modernization in China and Japan* (Belmont, Calif.: Wadsworth, 1995).

5. Iokibe Makoto, "Japan's Civil Society: An Historical Overview," in Tadashi (ed.), *Deciding*, pp. 51–96.

6. Lucian W. Pye, "Civility, Social Capital, and Civil Society: Three Powerful Concepts for Explaining Asia," *Journal of Interdisciplinary History*, 29 (Spring 1999), 763–82.

7. Pye, "Civility."

8. Pye, "Civility," p. 779.

9. Pye, "Civility"; also Pye, *Asian Power and Politics: The Cultural Dimensions of Authority* (Cambridge: Harvard University Press, 1985).

10. Peter Moody, "East Asia: The Confucian Tradition and Modernization," in Howard J. Wiarda (ed.), *Non-Western Theories of Development* (Fort Worth: Harcourt Brace, 1999), pp. 20–43.

11. Daniel Pipes and Adam Garfinkle (eds.), *Friendly Tyrants: An American Dilemma* (New York: St. Martin's, 1991).

12. Moody, *Tradition and Modernization*.

13. Tadashi, *Deciding.*

14. Yoshida, "Rethinking the Public Interest."

15. Yoshida, "Japan's Civil Society."

16. Shin'icki, "Rethinking the Public Interest," p. 48.

17. Ksunhyuk Kim, "Civil Society in South Korea: From Grand Democracy Movements to Petty Interest Groups," *Journal of Northeast Asian Studies* (Summer 1996), 81–97; Baogang He, "The Ideas of Civil Society in Mainland China and Taiwan," *Issues and Studies* (June 1995), 24–64; Yang May-sing, "NGOs Promote a Civil Society," *Taipei Journal* (October 27, 2000), p. 7.

6

LATIN AMERICA

Latin America has been one of the areas where the international civil society community has concentrated its assistance efforts. Latin America offers various advantages in these regards: (1) it is (like East Asia) a rapidly developing area; (2) it has a long history of republicanism and efforts to establish a functioning democracy and civil society; (3) democracy is the preferred form of government as indicated by public opinion surveys; and (4) United States influence in the area and that of its myriad NGOs and civil society groups is enormous. Latin America is, therefore (like South Africa), an important test case; if democracy and civil society cannot be established there, they are unlikely to be established anywhere.

And, in fact, in the past quarter-century, both democracy and civil society have advanced in Latin America. Along with Southern Europe, Latin America was one of the first, primary, and pioneering areas in the so-called "third wave" of global democratization. Nineteen of the twenty countries of the area (all except Cuba) are at least formally democratic. In general, the human rights situation in Latin America is considerably better in most countries than it was under the military authoritarianism of a generation ago. In addition, during this same period, with U.S. prodding and assistance, there has been a major growth in civil society.[1]

Yet, even with all this development, the situation neither of democracy nor of civil society is entirely comfortable or secure in

Latin America. First, while democracy has been formally established in almost all the countries, its substance—genuinely liberal and pluralist democracy—is still largely absent. Second, democracy is not well institutionalized; moreover, its popularity is declining, and in several countries support for "strong government" or authoritarianism now is larger than for democracy. Third, democracy has not delivered on many of its promises or improved social and economic conditions for the poor; in fact, social inequality in Latin America is worse now under democracy than it was earlier. Similarly with civil society: it has grown formally and in numbers of groups but it is not certain that has strengthened democracy, stability, or pluralism, which are, of course, the expressed goals of civil society. Instead, the suspicion is strong that rather than strengthening democracy, the increase in civil society may have mainly led to greater division, fragmentation, and instability.[2] Witness the cases of Argentina and Venezuela.

Furthermore, a considerable part of the growth of civil society has been opportunistic: Latin American elites, knowing that this is what the United States and the international community wanted, and that there was money available, have latched onto the civil society agenda, as onto other panaceas in the past, as a way of qualifying for grants and pleasing the international donors, meanwhile advancing their own private interests (as distinct from the public interest), giving the appearance of democracy and pluralism more than its substance, and in the process perhaps adding to the divisionism, chaos, fragmentation, and potential instability of their countries. In short, it is felt that, in Latin America as in other developing, non-Western nations, the growth of civil society is a somewhat artificial creation, financed and imported from the outside, without strong indigenous roots, and perhaps in the long run subversive of real democracy and stability rather than supportive of them.

SOCIOECONOMIC DATA

Latin America, for the most part, occupies an intermediate level in the world's rankings of socioeconomic development. Table 6.1 shows that it is neither so rich as the United States, Western Europe, or Japan, nor

Table 6.1   Latin American Indicators of Socioeconomic Development

Country	GNP	GNP per capita	Life expectancy		Literacy		Urban Percent	GNP per capita rank
			Male	Female	Male	Female		
Argentina	277.9	7,600	70	77	97	97	90	56
Bolivia	8.2	1,010	60	64	91	78	62	151
Brazil	742.8	4,420	63	71	84	84	81	81
Chile	71.1	4,740	72	78	96	95	85	68
Colombia	93.6	2,250	67	73	91	91	73	88
Costa Rica	9.8	2,740	74	79	95	93	48	87
Dominican Republic	16.1	1,910	69	73	83	83	64	103
Ecuador	16.2	1,310	68	73	92	89	64	141
El Salvador	11.8	1,900	67	72	81	75	46	114
Guatemala	18.4	1,660	61	67	75	60	39	125
Haiti	3.6	460	51	56	50	46	35	170
Honduras	4.8	760	67	72	73	73	52	148
Mexico	428.8	4,400	69	75	93	89	74	75
Nicaragua	2.1	430	66	71	66	69	56	152
Panama	8.6	3,070	72	76	92	91	56	98
Paraguay	8.5	1,580	68	72	94	94	55	111
Peru	60.3	2,390	66	71	94	94	72	107
Uruguay	19.5	5,900	70	78	97	98	91	70
Venezuela	87.0	3,670	70	76	93	91	87	94

Source: World Bank, *World Development Report*, 2000–2001

so poor as Africa and parts of the Middle East or Asia. The World Bank categorizes most of the Latin American countries as "middle income."

But that simple designation obscures a wide range of developmental levels and possibilities. Argentina is by far the wealthiest country in the area with a per-capita income (before its most recent crisis) approaching $8,000. Other relatively wealthy (at half the Argentine level) countries in the area include Brazil, Chile, Mexico, and Uruguay, in the $4,000–$5,000 per-person per-year range. But that is still only about *one-tenth* the level of the world's wealthiest nations. Moreover with a per-capita income level of under $400 (close to the African level) per year, Haiti and Nicaragua, the two poorest countries in Latin America, are at a level only one-tenth that of their wealthier, more hopeful neighbors, and only one one-hundredth that of the wealthiest nations. Most of the other countries are strung out between these poles, occupying middle-level positions.

Much the same applies to civil society. Civil society in Latin America is far less dense than it is in North America or Western Europe. On the other hand, it is considerably more developed than civil society in Africa and much of Asia and the Middle East. That is, there are political parties, labor unions, business groups, religious bodies, women's groups, peasant groups, organizations of indigenous persons, professional associations, social movements, community and neighborhood groups, and a variety of others. On the other hand, most of these groups are poorly organized and often ephemeral, have small memberships, are woefully underfunded and, therefore, very limited in their activities, and are not well institutionalized as pluralist and democratic bodies. In addition, most of them in one form and degree or another, are in a clientelistic or corporatist relationship with the state, either creations of it or dependent on it for recognition, funds, access, and entitlements.[3]

What is also striking about civil society in Latin America is that (1) there is little correlation between civil society and successful development or democratization, and (2) the growth of pluralism and civil society seems to lead not necessarily to stability but to division, fragmentation, and even political breakdown. In other words, the outcome of development in Latin America is not usually a happy, stable, pluralist, functioning democracy but instead conflict, polarization, and a form of morbific politics where the various groups are more often spinning in unconnected orbits or at each other's throats than working together toward common goals. If that is true, and if the pattern holds for other developing areas as well, it undermines virtually the entire argument advanced in favor of civil society and American (and other) assistance to it.

ELEMENTS OF POLITICAL CULTURE

Although both parts of the Americas share some aspects of a common history, in fact Latin America's traditions, culture, sociology, and, hence, politics are very different from those of North America. First of all, Latin America was founded on a pre-1500, pre-modern, medieval basis (closed, scholastic, hierarchical, authoritarian, absolutist, top-down, based on revealed truth), whereas the North American colonies, founded a century and more later, were founded on a modern or post-1500 basis. As Louis Hartz aptly states, the United States was "born free."[4]

Second, Latin America had a feudal past that the United States— except perhaps in the Old South—never did. Not only did Latin America have a feudal system of large estates, it also had a basically two-class system that, again apart from the South, the United States never had. Instead the United States was founded by basically middle-class elements, rural, self-sufficient, medium-sized family farmers, as well as urban commercial elements. The United States, unlike Europe or Latin America, never had a feudal past to overcome because it never had a feudal past, whereas much of Latin America's history since 1500 can be read as still striving to overcome the feudal structure left over from the past.

Third, Latin America's social structure, dominated by considerations of race and class, is much more rigid and unyielding than that of the United States. In the United States the colonists brought their families along and came to settle, whereas in Latin America the *conquistadores* came as conquerors without their families and were obliged to exploit the labor first of the native inhabitants and then of slaves imported from Africa. Society in North America, therefore, tends to be open and mobile whereas that of Latin America is far less open to those born poor and darker, far less amenable to rapid social mobility. U.S. society is basically fluid and middle class, whereas that of Latin America remained basically two-class and impenetrable.

Fourth, Latin America had far fewer resources—coal, iron ore, good coastal agricultural land, petroleum, internal river and transportation system—than did the United States and, therefore, fewer possibilities of economic development. What it did have was vast jungles, many areas of tropical and unhealthy climate, nonnavigable river systems, inhospitable mountains, and few areas amenable to development. Moreover, with its feudal, medieval past, Latin America had almost no entrepreneurial class, no middle class, no bourgeoisie. Its intellectual tradition, furthermore, was philosophical and scholastic rather than scientific and experimental, oriented toward preparing priests, lawyers, and philosophers but not engineers, agronomists, and scientists.

These factors help explain why Latin America lagged behind while the United States forged ahead. And why democracy and civil society in Latin America were also retarded in comparison with the United States

Now let us turn specifically to the cultural and intellectual tradition in explaining why, when civil society began to emerge, belatedly, in Latin America, it took a form very different from that of the United States.[5]

First, Latin America is a product of the Roman legal tradition, with its emphasis on the corporatist, organic, integral, hierarchical conception of law, as distinct from the common law tradition of Great Britain and the United States. Second, Latin America is heir to the historic Catholic-Thomistic conception of society, which similarly (and in a way that is mutually reinforcing) emphasizes a hierarchy of laws with different legal standards for different social strata, a similarly unified and organic (no checks and balances or countervailing interest groups) conception of society, a corporatist social order that emphasizes group rights over individual rights and locks each group into its proper station, a notion of authority that is God-given rather than popularly or democratically based, and a concept of leadership that is just but absolute. In the formative sixteenth and seventeenth centuries, when Latin America was indelibly imprinted and shaped, this meant an absolutist and authoritarian political system, a rigid, two-class, corporately organized social order, a centrally managed or mercantilist economy, an absolutist and intolerant religion, and a deductive, nonempirical system of law and learning.

When Latin America achieved independence in the early nineteenth century, its founding apostles were not Locke, Madison, and Jefferson in the U.S. liberal-pluralist tradition but, first, the Spanish neoscholastics in the Thomistic tradition and then the French philosopher

Rousseau. The neoscholastic roots of Latin American independence suggested more continuity with the past than change; indeed, Latin America's independence movements were conservative efforts to retain the status quo and not liberal, liberalizing, and progressive movements.

Rousseau was attractive because of his emphasis on strong, authoritative, if not authoritarian, leadership, the leader (like Augusto Pinochet or Fidel Castro) who *knows* the "general will" without having to check with the electorate, who by vision and force of personality enables a country to leapfrog over distinct socioeconomic stages or prerequisites to join the modern, progressive world without having to go through any intermediary steps. Especially important for our purposes was Rousseau's and, hence, Latin America's hostility to any and all intermediary organizations or what we would call civil society. Like Marx a century later, Rousseau saw such intermediaries as getting in the way of effective leadership, as serving as an inappropriate check on the general will, and as, therefore, frustrating national development. To this day, the Catholic-neoscholastic-Rousseauian tradition serves as a brake on civil society growth in Latin America; and anyone who wishes to assist such civil society development had better be prepared to come to grips with this tradition, which is very different from the liberal-pluralist North American one.

There are, of course, other reasons besides the intellectual and cultural ones for the slow growth of civil society in Latin America. These include, because of the rigidly centralized Spanish and Portuguese colonial systems, the almost complete lack of institutions or of training in democracy prior to independence. Another factor is the vast, near-empty, unruly (or "barbaric," as they are called in Domingo Sarmiento's classic of Latin American historical sociology) spaces, which seemed to call forth the compensatory need for strong, forceful, perhaps authoritarian leadership. A third factor is Latin America's underdeveloped status, its rigid class structure, its lack of institutions, and its feudal socioeconomic background—all of which retarded civil society development.

Implied in the preceding discussion are two overarching conclusions. The first is that, if Latin America can get beyond feudalism, develop modern institutions, and overcome its underdeveloped status, then presumably civil society will have an opportunity to grow. This developmentalist perspective is what provides hope to the legion of activists seeking to assist civil society development in Latin America. But the second conclusion, based on history, culture, and the Latin American intellectual tradition, again very different from the North American one, is that even if Latin America changes sociologically and economically, its political and civil society situation will continue to look quite different from that of the United States. It is emphatically *not* the case that, as socioeconomic development goes forward, Latin American political institutions and civil society will necessarily or automatically come to resemble those of the United States It is these two contending approaches that lie at the heart of the debate over the future of civil society in Latin America.

SOCIOECONOMIC CHANGE AND CHANGING STATE-SOCIETY RELATIONS

Latin America, along with Southern Europe, has long been known as the "home" of state corporatism and authoritarianism. Going back to the Roman-Thomistic-neoscholastic-Catholic historical tradition of corporatism, Latin America's corporatist structures have long and pervasive, almost "natural" roots. Among the earliest corporatist institutions were the Roman Catholic Church, the armed forces, and the landed elites or oligarchy. These three groups formed the traditional, nineteenth-century triumvirate of power in Latin America; they also dominated or controlled the state structure, thus giving rise to a unified or "organic" system of state-society relations. Hence, when manifest or ideological corporatism came to Latin America in the 1930s and 1940s, usually imported in various permutations from Mussolini's Italy, Franco's Spain, and Salazar's Portugal, much of Latin America felt right "at home" with the new ideology since, de facto, the elites of the area had been practicing corporatism all along. Historic Latin American political culture, in other words, shaped by this tradi-

tion, was organicist, group-centered, and corporatist rather than liberal, pluralist, and democratic. The laws and constitutions, mainly because of the strong U.S. influence in the Western Hemisphere, often
resembled the U.S. Constitution, but the practice was much closer to
an even more powerful tradition of top-down state corporatism.[6]

Manifest, ideological corporatism in Europe in the 1930s and
1940s was not just a reflection of historic ways of organizing society
but also, perhaps mainly, a response to what was called "the social
question," the rise of organized labor and the threats to the historic
system of power that the emerging working class constituted. Corporatism in this sense sought to provide an answer and alternative to
the Marxist threat, as well as to liberal-pluralism and capitalism,
which in the depression decade of the 1930s, accompanied by widespread political crises, seemed to be disintegrating. Corporatism appeared to present an alternative, what I have elsewhere called "the
other great 'ism,'"[7] given the unacceptability (Marxism) or failure
(liberalism) of the other options. Corporatism also provided a means
by which the elite groups mentioned earlier could maintain their
control of power even while adjusting to change. This was a clear political strategy for, as the old saw has it, if you want to stay the same,
you also have to be willing to change.

Historically in Latin America, new groups could be accommodated
to this corporatist system by adding on a new corporatist pillar to the
old regime. Thus, in the late nineteenth, early twentieth century the
rising business-commercial-entrepreneurial class (often foreign
born) was accommodated in this way; in the 1920s and 1930s (depending on the country) it became the turn of the middle class or,
since it lacked consciousness as a class, the "middle sectors" to be
absorbed into the system. Argentina, Brazil, Chile, Mexico, and
Uruguay, the most developed countries in Latin America, were also
the countries with the largest middle class and, thus, led the way in
adding new pillars to the historic triumvirate of power.

These rising groups were absorbed into the system of power and decision making in Latin America not out of altruism, the goodness of
anyone's heart, or a sudden conversion to liberalism and democracy.

Rather, this adjustment was purely an accommodation to changing social and power conditions. An aspiring new group such as the middle class, in the classic formulation of Charles W. Anderson,[8] had to meet two basic conditions. First, it had to demonstrate a power capability sufficient to challenge or threaten the existing power structure. If it was unable to do that, it could be—and frequently was—suppressed by the traditional groups. Second, it had to agree, as a condition of its recognition as a legitimate power contender, that it would not seek total power, that it would moderate its demands on the system and not pursue a total or all-or-nothing strategy. In this way the new group would be afforded legitimacy and the benefits of the system even while the old groups were never destroyed and kept their power positions. The strategy was accommodationist, but it was also gradual, involved both carrots and sticks, and was part of a long-term, ongoing political process.

The "system" was not nearly so rigid and unchanging as we often imagine Latin America to be; on the other hand, it was not really liberal, pluralist, and democratic either. In Anderson's formulation it was characterized by multiple legitimate routes to power (revolution and the skillfully executed *coup d'etat* as well as elections), the frequent use of structured political violence to demonstrate a power capability (the general strike, the march on the presidential palace, police or military repression, peasant or worker uprisings), the unequal distribution of power (with economic elites and the armed forces usually having a preponderance), and a political process in which the balance of power was renegotiated on virtually an everyday basis. Unlike the U.S. system where elections are considered definitive, elections in Latin America carried only tentative and often temporary legitimacy; at the same time a regime that came to power through nonelectoral means (coup, revolution) could acquire legitimacy by the popularity and success of its policies *after* taking office. Politics in this system tended to be informal and often unstable by U.S. standards, but it was more-or-less functional in the Latin American context.

The political process consisted of a long-term, fusion-absorption series of adjustments by which new groups (business, middle class, labor, etc.) were continuously added to the system without old groups being eliminated. Only in Mexico from 1910 to 1920, Bolivia in 1952, Cuba in 1959, and Nicaragua during the 1980s was there a full-scale, social revolution in which the traditional groups (Church, oligarchy, army) were eliminated and supplanted—and even in three of these four the change was only temporary. For the rest, politics was generally patronage-dominated, in which power was concentrated in the presidency and the person who held that office, the several corporate groups jockeyed for advantage and favors, and the possibility was ever present for crisis, breakdown, and even civil war. But the process *was* systematic; there was order amidst what outsiders perceived as chaos.

While exhibiting norms of regularity and normality—frequently referred to as "creole" or "home-grown" politics—the process was also biased, mainly in favor of the elite groups. It was they who controlled the process through the recognition and thus legitimization of new groups. The system was more top-down (state- and elite-centered and -controlled) than bottom-up. Though new groups could be added to the system, the old groups remained powerful; the vertical or pillared structure of the corporate system also served to preserve hierarchy, authority, and centralization, and to prevent horizontal or revolutionary alliances within and between groups. It was a fiendishly clever and eminently successful way by which the elites in Latin America maintained power for some five hundred years.[9]

But over time and under the impact of modernization, the foundations of this system began to give way. The causes are generally familiar to anyone who knows the history of social change. They include rising literacy, urbanization, industrialization, economic growth and integration, accelerated social change, and the impact of the outside world culture (globalization). The traditional fatalistic values began to fade, the Church lost its grip on the beliefs of the population; the newer groups organized on a basis (Marxism, neo-liberalism) very different from and opposed to the old system; young people no longer accepted the mores of their parents; democracy had its impact and so did U.S. policy as well as leftist and revolutionary appeals. By the 1950s and 1960s this hallowed system was in severe crisis, as evidenced by the Castro revolution in Cuba, its widespread appeal throughout Latin America, and the sudden, Castro-inspired preoccupation with the area of U.S. policy.

One further explanation seems to be called for at this point. If the Latin American social and political process consisted of the constant addition of new corporate groups (business, middle class, professional associations, organized labor, students, state bureaucrats, organized peasants, women, domestics, the indigenous) to the political process, why did this not produce democracy and pluralism as in the United States? The answer lies in the elite and statist control of the process, the tentative and often reversible nature of elections, the vertical and segmented corporatist structures, the absence of genuine democracy and egalitarianism, the patron-client system of politics, and the absence of consensus on the fundamental ends of politics. As a result, development and modernization in Latin America produced not necessarily democracy and pluralism as in the United States and Western Europe but increasing fragmentation, an "invertebrated society" (José Ortega y Gasset's term),[10] divisionism, and ultimately paralysis, gridlock, and breakdown.

The most literate, developed, and modern country in Latin America, Argentina from the 1930s to the 1980s, is the classic case, but Chile, Uruguay, Peru, and other countries also broke down into division and fragmentation, ultimately producing a wave of military-authoritarian takeovers. In other words, modernization in the Latin American context failed to produce democracy or democratic pluralism but instead was correlated with fragmentation and breakdown. And as a corollary of that, it is significant that it was the *most developed* countries that led the way to crisis and crash, not the less developed. And if it is so that the more developed show the way and provide a model for the less developed, then the pattern of development in Latin America is truly worrisome.

The Argentine case is, therefore, especially critical. As the most modern, most developed country in Latin America, Argentina has more interest groups, more civil society, than any other country in the region. However, in Jorge Bustamante's now-classic study,[11] virtually all these groups were creatures of the state, funded by the state, sometimes created by the state for political purposes, and, therefore, dependent on the state and subordinated to it. This was not an independent, pluralist civil society but a corporatist one. In one form or another, virtually the entire Argentine population worked for the state or received subsidies, jobs, entitlements, and patronage from it—often multiple jobs and entitlements. This included not just the usual corporatist groups—military, Church, labor, etc.—but also writers, professors, filmmakers, artists, lawyers, intellectuals, doctors, everyone.

Moreover, civil society had reached a point of saturation where the whole population was mobilized and organized. However, there were few overlapping memberships or competing loyalties, which meant everyone went all-out for his own group. The system worked well in prosperous times when there was sufficient patronage to dole out to everyone. But in austere times Argentina turned into a Hobbesian war of all-against-all with each group competing for the meager rewards within the system. This competition was often violent, producing stalemate and crisis. The gaps between the groups were so wide— literally from communist to fascist—that there was little room for compromise. Moreover, *within* these vertical compartments that is Argentine society, different partisan groups would often battle— often literally in gunfights—with each other for control of the government patronage designated for that particular sector; at the same time the government would play off these groups against each other to get its favored factions in control, all the better thereby to control and manipulate them. Under the weight of all these compound pressures, the system came periodically from the 1930s to the present to a state of stalemate, near civil war, and breakdown into morbific politics. At that point the military would step in; it, in turn, would eventually be discredited; and the cycle of fragmentation leading to authoritarianism back to fragmentation would repeat itself.

This is definitely not what they envision when international civil society advocates advance their agenda. But as the Argentine, Latin American, Egyptian and Middle Eastern, and African cases surveyed here show, this is what frequently happens when civil society development takes place within a corporatist as distinct from a liberal-pluralist context. Furthermore, and we cannot stress the point enough, it is not the least developed but the most developed countries in the several regions—Argentina, Egypt, South Africa—that show the greatest tendency to fragment and break down in this way.

By the late 1970s, early 1980s, Latin America had tired of authoritarianism and repression and embarked anew on its periodic quest for democracy. The question is whether the historic cyclical pattern indicated above—authoritarianism leading to repression which leads to disillusionment, leading to renewed calls for democracy, then fragmentation, civil conflict, and gridlock leading to demands again for order, unity, and "strong government"—will once again be repeated, or if conditions in Latin America have changed sufficiently for the older cycle to be broken and democracy established on a stronger basis. At least four factors of change lead us to be more hopeful now than previously about democracy's prospects.

First, Latin America has changed dramatically since the last, failed effort at democratization forty years ago. It is more urban, developed, literate, middle class; less Catholic, oligarchic, military dominated, traditionalist. It is more integrated into global affairs and markets, more influenced by the global culture (including the preference for democracy and human rights), and more a part of the modern, Western, democratic world. Second, Latin America has benefitted from the end of the Cold War, which has reduced tensions and conflict in the area, led to the decline in support for revolutionary forces, many of which have now become part of the democratic process, and allowed the powerful, brooding, often interventionist power to the north, the United States, to concentrate on other, more positive issues besides anti-communism. Third and related, democracy in Latin America has been strengthened by the emphasis, on the part of a host of U.S. institutions (AID, State Department, Defense Department, the two major parties, election monitors, NGOs), on assisting democracy development in Latin America. And fourth, democracy has been enhanced by the lack of popularity/discrediting of the other main alternatives (both Marxism and authoritarianism) and the widespread sense that, worldwide, democracy is the only legitimate "game in town."[12]

The questions we need to wrestle with here are whether the third wave of democratization in Latin America has undermined corporatist and statist structures and, relatedly, whether civil society has been correspondingly strengthened, establishing a firmer basis for democracy. Several conclusions may be tentatively stated, allowing for considerable variation between countries:

1. In the last twenty years most countries have, at least legally and formally, abolished or liberalized their corporatist structures to allow greater freedom of associational life.

2. Throughout Latin America civil society is considerably stronger than it was a generation ago.

3. Political parties and interest groups are now generally free to organize and carry out their activities without government or military interference.

4. There are new social movements of women, peasants, the indigenous, slum-dwellers, and other groups that have achieved considerable influence and at this stage would be difficult for any government to repress.

5. Civil society has been instrumental in several notable cases in staving off coups, securing honest elections, pressuring for reform, and taking the lead in numerous policy areas.

6. Democratic elections (no longer coups or revolutions) are widely considered the only legitimate route to power.

7. International NGOs have been particularly active in fostering civil society in Latin America.

8. Latin American elites, seeing the handwriting on the wall, have moved to fill the organizational space by creating their own (often official or co-opted) civil society.

These are hopeful signs, but we also need to keep in mind:

1. While legally and formally abolishing corporatism, most governments, such as in Brazil, still maintain some limits, controls, and registration and recognition requirements on interest-group activity.

2. Civil society groups are often the creations of outside or foreign groups on whom they are absolutely dependent for support; when the support goes, the civil society group often folds as well.

3. Political parties, interest groups, and institutions in general remain weak, poorly organized, often patronage dominated, and corrupt.

4. Many of the new social movements are agencies of the state, of political parties, or of powerful patrons and elites, and not truly autonomous.

5. Civil society is often biased politically; most civil society groups are on the activist, progressive, reformist, left side of the political spectrum.

6. While the state is "letting go" of its corporate controls in some policy areas, it is creating new public-private "partnerships" in these same areas as a way of maintaining control while appearing to liberalize.

7. Similarly, while corporate controls are being formally abolished at national levels, they are often being re-created at local levels where authorities are increasingly forcing NGOs and civil society groups to register, reveal their financial sources, show their membership lists, and seek juridical recognition, which, of course, gives local authorities the power also to deny or postpone recognition.

8. Civil society in Latin America, as in East Asia and Central/Eastern Europe, tends to mobilize around a single coherent issue (overthrow of authoritarianism, democratic elections, specific policy arenas); when that issue is resolved (which is also when the outside funding usually dries up), civil society also goes into remission. The evidence for a permanent, standing civil society is weak.

9. Mexico is a key country and one of our important case studies.[13] For seventy years it had a corporatist-authoritarian, but civilian-dominated, single-party regime, recently undergoing liberalization. Here the situation of civil society is even more complex:

(a) Corporatist organizations linked to the state or long-time dominant party are locked in competition with new, rising, liberal civil society.

(b) The state is attempting to maintain its control over the corporatist structure while also, alternatively, giving free rein to or controlling the newer liberal associations.

(c) To compete in this new, more liberal context, corporatist organizations are also reforming from within, becoming more populist, loosening the control aspects.

(d) Meanwhile, the state itself has changed hands, from the long–dominant Revolutionary Institutional Party (PRI) to Vicente Fox and the opposition National Action Party, providing for greater pluralism and competition among groups.

(e) There is enormous pressure from the United States and its civil society groups, as well as within Mexico, for further liberalization of associational life.

(f) When the Mexican economy is doing well, free associability tends to increase; when the economy performs badly and social tensions increase, the pressures for greater controls over group life (re-corporatization) also increase.

(g) New groups—Indians, women, peasants, slum-dwellers, *many* others—are also mobilizing as *independent* social movements, with each group trying to retain its autonomy (but looking for government entitlements), while the state attempts to co-opt, capture, and control it.

(h) Many foreign-based NGOs have been established in Mexico. Some of these have blatantly intervened, for example in support of the Zapatista Indian movement, in Mexican internal political affairs, prompting a major debate within the Mexican government whether to ignore them, force them to register corporatist-style (difficult to do with foreign NGOs), or expel them.

(i) The overall result is both a more democratic *and* a more chaotic, fragmented Mexico than in the past. When the economy is strong, democratic prospects look good; when the economy falters, it gives rise to a zero-sum game of intense competition among all groups for the declining patronage and entitlements, and fragmentation becomes more severe, leading to the potential for breakdown.

THE INTERNATIONAL CONTEXT

Latin America has been one of the main areas, maybe *the* main area, where foreign or outside civil society groups have concentrated their efforts. In part that is because Latin America is close to the United States; in part it is due to the fact that Latin America, like Sub-Saharan Africa, has long been treated both as an outpost for missionarylike proselytizing, in this case for such secular goals as democracy and civil society, and as a guinea pig or laboratory for social and political experimentation and engineering.[14]

In the last decade the "missionaries" for civil society, mainly U.S.-based but some European as well, have swarmed into Latin America to mobilize new groups, teach "good government" U.S.-style to the "natives," and to lobby on behalf of numerous "good causes," including anti-corruption, judicial reform, counter-narcotics, education reform, privatization and neoliberalism, decentralization and local government, election reform, tax reform, military reform, and a *host* of others. The number, range, and all-encompassing nature of these reform efforts are reminiscent of the 1960s and the Peace Corps, missionarylike attitudes of those times when U.S. AID and the other U.S. missions all but ran and took over many of the Latin American countries.

The issue is not whether these reforms are good for Latin America; many of them are. Rather, the questions are whether the many foreign groups and persons operating in Latin America know what they are doing, whether they understand Latin American realities and ways of doing things, whether they are sufficiently sensitive to Latin American culture and practices or insist, with their global, universal agendas, on running roughshod over them; and, hence, whether, in their zeal to accomplish their goals, they do more harm than good. The record of such missionaries and "do-gooders" in Latin America is not a glorious one, but of course they can also leave when their experiments go astray or produce unintended consequences, leaving Latin Americans to cope with or clean up the problems they often leave behind.

It is difficult for Latin America, especially the smaller countries, to cope with this onslaught of civil society advocates. In part that is so because they are usually well meaning and the programs they champion apparently quite noble, in part it is due to the fact that loans and grants from U.S. agencies and the major international lending banks are often conditioned on going along with the programs the civil society groups advocate, in part it is due to the sheer wealth, power, Wall Street connections, and presumed know-how of the foreign-based groups that tend to be overwhelming in poor, weak, dependent countries.

When faced with the invasion (the term sounds harsh but that is often what it amounts to) of these foreign civil society armies and their lavish (compared to the host countries) budgets, Latin American countries have a variety of ways of coping. Mostly they simply go along with the foreign groups either because they agree with the agenda and the solutions offered, or because they think it is futile and self-defeating to resist. Only in special cases would the small "sardines" (the Latin American countries) take on the "shark" (the United States) of the north. But often the country disagrees with the agenda and the proposed solutions, or it has other priorities, or it sees the issue in a different light.

Then, it has a variety of options. One, and the most common, is to pass the formal legislation required, so as to give the appearance of compliance (and thereby also qualifying for all-important IMF and World Bank loans), but then not implement, foot-drag, or implement only partially. A second government option is to simply turn over certain programs to the international civil society groups and let them manage them as a way of keeping them both busy and happy, meanwhile keeping the more important arenas of patronage, economy, and armed forces decision making in the government's own hands. A third option, increasingly used, is the corporatist strategy of forcing even foreign-based civil society groups to register, file their membership lists, show where the money comes from, and seek a grant of juridical "personality" or recognition from the state. A fourth option, also increasingly used but selectively, is, as in Mexico, to expel the civil society groups from the country.

In *all* my case study countries I sensed growing tension between the governments involved and the foreign-based civil society groups. The civil society groups are often welcomed for their money and because indigenous reformers agree with their agenda or do not wish to see their country branded a pariah on the international stage. But they are deeply resented for their interference in the internal affairs of the host nation, for their arrogance ("we know best"), for their insensitivity to local conditions, and frequently for their anti-government activities. This is a tension that has existed in virtually all U.S. AID efforts since the early 1960s; on the part of the receiving countries, experience has taught that after a few years this latest international panacea will also pass and, in the meantime, one should accept the money, make some, usually feeble efforts toward reform, and wait for the international donors' enthusiasm to run its course and then go on to other things.

CONCLUSION

The rise of civil society, often locally grown but aided and abetted from the outside, was undoubtedly influential two decades ago in the critically important transition of Latin America from authoritarianism to democracy. Moreover, in many countries civil society remains vibrant and important in securing democracy against threats, guaranteeing honest elections, and initiating reform in new policy arenas. New social movements similarly continue to mobilize new voices and social groups. These are important functions and activities, and the role of civil society in accomplishing them is great. Civil society continues to be a bulwark of democracy even in the present period of declining support for democracy, and an essential leader and booster of many necessary reform agendas.

As in other regional areas examined here, however, civil society as a critical force has declined since the large issue-of-the-moment of democratization was successfully accomplished. In part this is due to "natural" forces: when authoritarianism was in power, civil society was often the only opposition to it; but now that democracy has been reestablished, political parties, interest groups, government institutions, and other informal channels of influence have reasserted themselves, diminishing the role of civil society. In part also, it is due to the longtime Latin American sense of discomfort and unease with an unregulated, uncontrolled, *laissez-faire* and liberal-pluralist political system. Hence, the felt need oftentimes to continue to regulate, control, and corporatize group activities, to rein in what to Latin Americans often seems to be an anarchic, chaotic, free associability. Hence, the drive to limit, to manage, and to oversee civil society and group life for "the common good."

To the extent that civil society is home-grown and emerges naturally, organically, and more or less in accord with Latin American development processes, it is widely supported. But to the extent it is artificial, imported, imposed from the outside, and not in accord with Latin America's culture or level of development (which, of course, also varies by country), it will not be supported. In the latter case, Latin America will go through the motions, accept the money of the foreign NGOs but little of the substance of their reform proposals, meanwhile trying to limit and control the activities these groups spawn. This is, therefore, a complex picture: civil society is supported at some levels and in some circumstances, in others it is rejected, diminished, reined in. So rather than a consensus around civil society, in Latin America it continues to be a source of multiple tensions.

NOTES

1. For background and an optimistic view, see Howard J. Wiarda, *Latin American Politics: A New World of Possibilities* (Belmont, Calif.: Wadsworth, 1994).

2. Howard J. Wiarda and Harvey F. Kline, *An Introduction to Latin American Politics and Development* (Boulder: Westview Press, 2001), for a later, more pessimistic outlook.

3. Jorge Bustamante, *La República Corporativa* (Buenos Aires: EMECE Editors, 1988).

4. Louis Hartz, *The Liberal Tradition in America* (New York: Harcourt, Brace, Jovanovich, 1957); for the Latin American contrast see Richard M. Morse, *New World Soundings: Culture and Ideology in the Americas* (Baltimore: Johns Hopkins University Press, 1989).

5. Howard J. Wiarda, *The Soul of Latin America* (New Haven: Yale University Press, 2001).

6. James Malloy (ed.), *Authoritarianism and Corporatism in Latin America* (Pittsburgh: University of Pittsburgh Press, 1977).

7. Howard J. Wiarda, *Corporatism and Comparative Politics* (New York: M. E. Sharpe, 1997a).

8. Charles W. Anderson, *The Governing of Restless Nations: Politics and Economic Change in Latin America* (Princeton: D. Van Nostrand, 1967).

9. Howard J. Wiarda and Harvey F. Kline (eds.), *Latin American Politics and Development* (Boulder: Westview Press, 2000), Introduction.

10. José Ortega y Gasset, *Invertebrate Spain* (New York: Norton, 1937).

11. Bustamante, *República Corporativa*.

12. Howard J. Wiarda, *The Democratic Revolution in Latin America* (New York: The Twentieth Century Fund, Holmes and Meier, 1990).

13. Suzanne Bilello, "Mexico: The Rise of Civil Society," *Current History* (February 1996), 82–87; Alberto J. Olvera, "Civil Society and Political Transition in Mexico," *Constellations* 4, 1 (1997), 105–23; Neil Harvey (ed.), *Mexico: Dilemmas of Transition* (New York: St. Martin's, 1993).

14. Thomas Carothers, *Aiding Democracy Abroad* (Washington, D.C.: Carnegie Endowment, 1999); Carothers and Marina Ottaway (eds.), *Funding Virtue: Civil Society Aid and Democracy Promotion* (Washington, D.C.: Carnegie Endowment, 2000).

7

THE MIDDLE EAST
AND ISLAMIC SOCIETY*

Of all the world's areas, the Middle East has been the most disappointing in terms of economic and social development, democratization, and the growth of civil society. Note we said "most disappointing," not "least successful"; the latter dubious designation belongs to Sub-Saharan Africa. The Middle East is the most disappointing in the sense that, given its resources (mainly oil wealth), proximity to other wealthy areas (the European Union), population, and potential, it should be more developed than it is. It should be up there with East Asia or Latin America as an emerging, increasingly affluent, more democratic set of nations with strong civil society. But, in fact, most countries of the area lag behind.

Look at the figures in Table 7.1. Almost all the countries are at the low end of the scale in terms of per-capita income, life expectancy, literacy (especially for women), percent urbanized, and overall ranking. *Nowhere* in the region do we see any Big Emerging Markets (BEMs) such as Argentina, Brazil, Chile, China, Indonesia, Mexico, South Korea, or Taiwan (note all these are from Latin America or East Asia). Israel is the only developed country in the region; it is also the only non-Islamic country. *None* of the Middle Eastern

---

*Written before September 11, 2001.

countries—again excepting Israel—is a democracy or has a democratic, pluralist, participatory civil society.

The questions are why and whether the sad situation of democracy and civil society in the Middle East is likely to change any time soon. Among the competing explanations are Islamic political culture, on the one hand: Is there something in Islamic political culture that tends to discourage or retard democracy and civil society? On the other hand, is it the low level of socioeconomic development; if that is the key factor, then presumably once development occurs, democracy and civil society would also spring forth. A third possible explanation is the class structure and antiquated, two-class social system of the Middle East. And finally there are what are called "dependency factors": the Middle East's position on the periphery of the world's more affluent areas, its dependent position in the world economy, and its location as a center of Cold War conflicts, Arab-Israeli hatreds, terrorism, and internecine warfare.[1] As we go through the following discussion, we will seek to analyze these competing explanations and sort out which offers the more cogent explanation.

SOCIOECONOMIC DATA

The data presented in Table 7.1 show that the countries of the Middle East, with a few exceptions, are among the world's poorest, least-developed countries. They are not as poor as those in Africa who often rank below the $1,000 per-capita per-year income level and have lower levels of life expectancy, literacy, and urbanization. But they are below the level of the emerging Latin American countries and *way below* the rapidly developing countries of East Asia and Central/Eastern Europe. Lebanon is the only (non-oil) country that approaches the $4,000 per-person per-year level (about one-tenth of the world's richest countries); most of the countries of the area are in the $1,000–$2,000 range. Bahrain, Oman, Qatar, Kuwait, Saudi

Table 7.1 Middle East/Islamic Indicators of Socioeconomic Development

Country	GNP	GNP per capita	Life expectancy		Literacy		Urban Percent	GNP per capita rank
			Male	Female	Male	Female		
Afghanistan		775 or less[a]	46		35			Low income
Algeria[b]	46.5	1,550	69	72	76	54	60	101
Bahrain		2,996–9,265[a]	73		86			Upper middle income
Egypt	87.5	1,400	65	68	65	42	45	127
Iran	110.5	1,760	70	72	82	67	61	95
Iraq		756–2,995[a]	59		54			
Israel		9,266 or more[a]	76	80	98	94	91	Lower middle income
Jordan	7.0	1,500	69	73	94	83	74	124
Kuwait		9,266 or more[a]	74	80	78	10	97	
Lebanon	15.8	3,700	68	72	91	79	89	76
Libya		2,996–9,265[a]	70		78			Upper middle income
Morocco	33.8	1,200	65	69	60	34	55	131
Oman		2,996–9,265[a]	73		69			Upper middle income
Pakistan	64.0	470	61	63	58	29	36	159
Qatar		9,226 or more[a]	74		80			High income
Saudi Arabia		2,996–9,265[a]	70	74	83	64	85	59
Syria	15.2	970	67	72	87	58	54	139
Tunisia	19.9	2,100	70	74	79	58	65	91
Turkey	186.3	2,900	67	72	93	75	74	134
United Arab Emirates		9,266 or more[a]	75		75			High income
Yemen	5.9	350	55	56	66	23	24	197

SOURCE: World Bank, *World Development Report, 2000–2001.*

[a]Estimates by World Bank.

[b]Following custom, the Islamic countries of North Africa are included in the "Middle East" category

Arabia, and the United Arab Emirates are anomalies: because they almost literally float on oil they have comparatively higher per-capita income levels even while retaining antiquated social structures that are not conducive to democracy or democratic civil society. Turkey's relatively higher level of development is explainable by its proximity to wealthy Europe, its sizable resources and population, its internal modernization, and hence the growth of a more modern secular state, and Turkey's increased integration into European markets. Nevertheless, Israel remains the only country in the area that is (1) developed, (2) fully democratic, and (3) with pluralist and democratic civil society.

The main question for us is, as the Middle East develops both economically and sociologically (becoming more urban, literate, and prosperous), will it also become more democratic and with a stronger civil society? The answer is, probably yes. The fact is that some countries of the region (Algeria, Egypt, Jordan, Lebanon, Morocco, Pakistan, Tunisia), as they have developed, have also introduced some, often limited or sporadic democratic reforms and openings, such as greater respect for human rights, elections, a parliament. Generally, these are the more prosperous countries as well, so there *is* a correlation in the Middle East (as elsewhere) between development and democracy. But the correlation is not strong and there may be (as in several of the countries listed) reversions to more authoritarian practices.

No country of the area (except Israel, obviously a special case) has become fully democratic. Nor do we have a single country in the Middle East like South Korea or Taiwan, where economic development became so strong that it almost *forced* an existing, authoritarian regime to democratize. In addition, we have countries like Algeria, Iran, Iraq, Libya, Syria, and others where economic and social development failed to spawn democracy, instead producing only stronger authoritarian governments or Islamicist regimes hostile to democracy. Meanwhile, countries like Afghanistan and Yemen, both low (close to Haiti) in the per-capita income rankings and also with almost no background or bases for democracy, have shown little progress either economically or politically.

ELEMENTS OF POLITICAL CULTURE

Islamic political culture has not historically been strongly supportive of democracy and civil society. Reinforced by and often themselves manipulating the political culture for their own private political or personal ends, governments of the region have not usually been very tolerant either of opposition political movements or of a pluralistic associational life outside of their control. They have moved to quash both opposition political parties as well as interest organizations that they could not control. Within the region only Israel has consistently maintained its democratic character; Turkey has moved in that direction; Pakistan has practiced democracy sporadically, while in Jordan and Kuwait some limited steps have been taken to open up the political system even while keeping the opposition under tight control. Intimidation often coupled, in the best of circumstances, with co-optation has been the main system of control.

Neither the *Koran* nor the *Shariah* (holy law) offers much justification for democracy or civil society. Instead, there is abundant rationalization of top-down, authoritarian, male-dominated decision making. Just as Allah is God and all things are subordinated to that fundamental principle, so the family, the essential and basic unit of society, is headed by the father/husband, the tribe or clan is similarly dominated by authoritarian leadership, and political authority at the state level is also concentrated, centralized, and top-down. *Nowhere* is there grounds for grassroots participation from below, although the leader, whether in the family, the tribe, or the nation-state, is supposed to consult broadly with society.[2]

For example, in Saudi Arabia, King Fahd would regularly pack his tent, assemble his entourage, and head out into the desert to consult with the bedouin chiefs. He would also find time to take petitions from humble people. If possible, he or his staff would take care of the problem on the spot; if that was not possible, the issue would be dealt with by appropriate government agencies immediately upon returning to Riyadh. This is obviously not democracy, but it does provide for some degree of consultation and participation. Petitions may be granted but the manner and system of doing so serves to reinforce the clientelistic, hierarchical, and authoritarian elements in the society.

It is clear that to the extent the *Koran* and *Shariah* talk about governance at all (not a great deal), they tend to justify authoritarian rule. It is also clear that authoritarian leaders have learned to take advantage of these holy injunctions for their own advantage. Between the God-given justifications for authoritarianism, on the one hand, and its long practice, on the other, authoritarianism is by now so deeply imprinted in Islamic society that it is part of the political culture, the normal way of doing things. And once it is *that* deeply a part of the political culture, the harder—almost impossible—it becomes to change. On the other hand, as Anwar Syed points out, *nowhere* in the *Koran* or *Shariah* is there any express prohibition against democracy.[3] That fact opens the possibility for democracy and elections in the future as we have seen even in such Muslim cleric-dominated societies as Iran, where more-or-less democratic elections have recently been held.

Much the same applies to human rights. Human rights in the Western sense have not often been rigorously observed in Islamic society; on the contrary, the Muslim countries are known—and condemned—for the excesses (stoning to death), cruelty (the cutting off of the hands of robbers), and arbitrariness of their criminal law, itself shaped powerfully by Islamic precepts. The religious-cultural-historical setting has not been conducive to democracy and human rights.

Most regimes in the area have not been supportive of democracy, have seldom opened up to democracy, and have been suspicious of civil society. What civil society exists has been weak and frail. Governments have sought to regulate it closely, control it, and keep it from posing potentially a threat to the regime in power. These regimes, in the Middle East as well as in East Asia and Latin America, have been almost inherently corporatist.

The civil society that is present has been all but exclusively limited to the male proportion of the population. Women have been subordinated: in the home and in family affairs they are influential, but not in the public sphere, where women's groups are largely nonexistent or very small in numbers. Moreover, there is here as elsewhere in the Third World a class bias in civil society; most civil society groups are composed of upper- and upper-middle-class elements. In contrast, labor, peasant, bedouin, and urban slum-dweller groups are seldom organized or, if they are, they are tightly regulated by the government.

Clientelism tends to pervade all levels of society, bureaucracy, and relations with state agencies. Clientelism, with its system of supplicants, on the one hand, and patrons, on the other, is almost everywhere inherently unequal and undemocratic. Everyone in one way or another is tied into this top-to-bottom clientelistic system. Whom you know is more important than what you know. To those who do have the right connections, patronage may take the form of jobs, favors, special access, government contracts, whole programs, and even government ministries doled out to the "deserving" in return for loyalty and support. As society becomes more organized and differentiated, the clientelistic system is extended to whole groups in society and no longer just individuals. Once again we are back to corporatism, for when a group's relations with the state are grounded on a clientelistic, patronage-based, subordinate-superordinate basis, that is a formula for corporatism.

Some have argued that civil society in the Middle East should be seen as not less developed than that of the West but only *different* from it, and I accept that argument—up to a point. Historically, civil society in the Middle East has consisted of three main groups: the clergy (*ulema*), tribes and tribal confederations, and traditional merchants (*bazaris*).[4] By Islamic law as well as precedence, the king or ruler is obliged to consult with these groups. But (1) this is an exceedingly narrow range of interests with which to consult, rather like the three European estates (clergy, nobles, and common) of the Middle Ages; (2) it does not take into consideration new and modernizing groups such as labor unions, professionals, or women; and (3) such a system of personalistic, clientelistic consultation provides little training or experience in the functioning of a modernizing democracy.

Another problem is that, as civil society has begun to emerge in the Middle East, it has taken a form that most Westerners are quite uncomfortable with. For example, in a number of countries the claim has been put forward—often by military officers and their not-very-democratic civilian supporters—that the armed forces, which are at or near the surface of power in most Middle Eastern countries, should be considered a part—maybe *the* part—of civil society. A second candidate for civil society status is the family, meaning the extended family and usually implying (although seldom said publicly) the ruling family and its various hangers-on, clientelistic relations, sycophants, and bureaucratic interests. A third group is the tribe or clan, which in some writings is being elevated to the status of a modernizing agency because it delivers some, limited public goods and services; but, as in Africa, it is sometimes hard for objective observers to think of "tribe" as a modern, public-interested, civil society group.

But the most troubling debate revolves around the issue of Islamic fundamentalism. Many Islamic societies have been undergoing a religious revival of late, secularism that was once associated with modernization appears to be in decline, and the Islamic fundamentalist movements are being touted as the Muslim world's civil society, the Islamic answer and counterpart to the hated liberalism, secularism, and supposed moral degeneracy of the West. Islamic fundamentalism in Afghanistan, Iran, Algeria, Pakistan, and increasingly Egypt and other countries as well has now taken the form of a mass movement, mobilized millions of followers, toppled or threatened to topple a score of governments, and promised to install a strict Islamic regime hostile to other forms of worship, to free speech, and to Western liberal ideals.

Islamic fundamentalism seems to fit almost all our definitions of civil society, yet in its illiberal views it is unacceptable to most Westerners. In this sense it is rather like the Ku Klux Klan, various American militias, or the German skinheads: undoubtedly a part of civil society but not exactly what most of us have in mind by that term. This case (and that of tribalism in Africa or caste associations in India) provides one of the acid tests of our cultural relativism and commitment to civil society in whatever form. Can we accept a form of civil society that most of us abhor, or does our adherence to Western values in this case take precedence over our commitment to civil society?[5]*

The literature on Islamic fundamentalism, to say nothing of a prudent foreign policy, suggests that some further distinctions need to be made. We may, for example, accept the fact that an Islamic revival is occurring in the Muslim world without necessarily welcoming all the movements spawned by it. There are, after all, a variety of Islamic voices on these themes and not just a single monolithic voice. Specifically, we need to distinguish between Islamic fundamentalist movements that are peaceful and show promise of moderation and democracy, versus those that employ terrorism and are violently opposed to Western liberal values. Clearly we can accommodate to the former while rejecting the latter. For if in the United States and other Western societies we accept the idea that religious movements, churches, synagogues, and now mosques form one part of civil society, we should also be prepared to accept the idea of Islamic fundamentalism as a part of civil society in the Middle East.

It is useful, by making these distinctions, to remain hopeful about both Islamic democracy and the possibilities of a viable, home-grown civil society to undergird it. But we also need to be realistic: some of this hope may be grasping at straws. For the overwhelming weight of Islamic culture and history, so far, has not been supportive of democracy or of a liberal, pluralist civil society. Rather, virtually the whole of Islamic history and culture has been authoritarian, top-down, and elitist. Some favored groups are advantaged whereas others are left behind. Social and political structures tend to be feudal and sultanic rather than modern and democratic. The system of clientelism and patron-client relations that reaches from the lowest to

---

*Although the present author is known in the scholarly world as something of a cultural relativist, I had long ago decided that I was not in favor of an Iranian regime that kidnaps Americans, an Afghanistan regime that is oppressive, a Sudanese regime that slaughters Christians, or an Algerian rebel movement that slits sleeping people's throats in the middle of the night. One can recognize that different societies and cultures do things in different ways even while holding firm to one's own cherished values.

highest levels is inherently undemocratic, and as the Middle East has gradually modernized and developed over the years, that clientelistic system has also modernized and become more institutionalized rather than being displaced by democracy. The weight of history, culture, and religion in the Middle East is, therefore, extremely heavy, maybe even weightier than in East Asia and Latin America, and *almost none* of this heavy hand is propitious for democracy or democratic civil society.[6]

SOCIOECONOMIC CHANGE AND CHANGING STATE-SOCIETY RELATIONS

The presumption is that once socioeconomic change in the developing world begins in earnest, it tends to give rise to a more diverse and broader-based civil society that in turn begets democracy. Economic growth, the argument runs, stimulates social differentiation and thereby vast social changes—a new business class, a middle class, organized labor, women's groups, others—that produce pluralism and thereby make democracy a necessity and not just a luxury. For only democracy and democratic pluralism, we now know, not Marxism-Leninism or authoritarianism, have the capacity and flexibility to handle the social changes brought on by modernization. Certainly that has been the pattern in South Korea, Taiwan, increasingly in other Asian societies, and Latin America as well: economic growth that stimulates social change that in turn makes democracy a pragmatic necessity.

But not in the Middle East. Or, to be more precise, not so much in the Middle East. There, not enough industrialization or economic growth has occurred to trigger such vast social changes—the first step in the process of democratization. Recall those per-capita income numbers from Table 7.1: the overwhelming majority of the countries of the area remain very poor. Only a handful—Egypt, Lebanon, Turkey—have had the kind of sustained economic growth to stimulate the vast social changes talked of here, giving rise to eventual societal pluralism and the hope for greater democracy. And those countries that do have a higher per-capita income—Kuwait, Oman, Qatar, Saudi Arabia, the United Arab Emirates—have such a distorted, even artificial-growth pattern under their feudal sultanates, most of which are probably doomed in long-range terms, that the normal, expected process of social differentiation and change has not occurred. Whether because of too little, too slow, or distorted growth, the Middle East has not seen yet the vast social transformation stimulating political pluralism and democratization that we saw in East Asia and Latin America.

Moreover, when they do begin to modernize socially, the form of civil society that emerges is generally corporatist rather than liberal and pluralist.[7] Egypt is perhaps the leading case study. Egypt is one of the most developed and most Westernized countries in the Middle East; it has also been the recipient of more U.S. foreign aid, aimed at stabilizing and democratizing it, than any other country in the world except Israel. Yet despite all this developmental assistance that has now gone on for over three decades, Egypt remains an authoritarian state and not a liberal one, corporately organized, and increasingly a police state.[8]

As Egypt (and other Middle East states) began to modernize, tribal, bedouin, and other traditional civil society groups began to lose influence. In their place came new urban groups: associations of journalists, lawyers, physicians, engineers, etc. Although the state has legally recognized and legitimized *some* of these newer groups, allowing them to play a limited social and political role, it has failed to recognize others and even repressed them. In addition, most of these groups are politically innocuous, reluctant to challenge or "take on" the state and its leaders, and both unwilling and incapable of mounting any opposition against the state for fear of losing the few corporatist privileges the state grants them. And, because of the corporatist system of organization, the groups do not compete with each other horizontally as in the pluralist model but instead are organized vertically, through the state, which weakens their power, prevents alliances from forming, and ties them to a relationship of dependence to the state. As Mehran Kamrava and Frank Mora conclude, the Middle Eastern states "have been able to maintain those corporatist arrangements through which they keep key social groups beholden to them."[9] So far at least, as modernization has proceeded, the Middle Eastern state has been able to keep its corporatist controls in place, even expanding them to encompass new groups, but seldom moving toward liberalism, let alone being overwhelmed by it.

A key actor in all these arrangements is organized labor. Labor and industrial relations have long been the anvil on which the shape and structure of the modern state have been pounded out.[10] But as an organized labor movement began to emerge in Egypt and other of the more developed Middle East countries, it was tied to the state and controlled by the state in corporatist rather than liberal-pluralist fashion. Organized labor was duly recognized by the state and received some benefits from it, but it also became a client (one among many) of the state and was carefully circumscribed in its activities. It was patronized by the state, kept subservient, sometimes roughed up by security forces, prevented from allying itself with other change-oriented groups, and severely limited (even outlawed at times) in its political activities. There are different interpretations of this phenomena: Louis Cantori emphasizes the corporatist control mechanisms,[11] while Marsha Pripstein Posusney argues that organized labor has been clever in achieving some limited benefits for its members even within these corporatist arrangements.[12] But everyone agrees that state-society relations in the Middle East are essentially corporatist ones rather than liberal-pluralist.

While this is the established and still ongoing structure of Egyptian state-society relations, a newer phenomenon (in the last thirty years) has been the rise of political Islam as an alternative form of civil society.[13] Egypt's grassroots Islamic movement, which is made up of lawyers, doctors, students, mullahs, and ordinary men and women, has grown enormously in recent years, penetrated the state, and increasingly challenged the government. One needs to distinguish between the armed revolutionary groups seeking to impose Islamic rule by force and that have gotten most of the publicity, and the "quieter," popular Islamic movements that are broad-based within the society. Particularly in the last decade the quieter Islamic activists have, mainly through democratic elections, taken over the key professional unions that represent hundreds of thousands of Egypt's educated, middle-class citizens. The Islamic groups have increasingly captured Egypt's corporately organized civil society groups, but they refuse to play by the old rules and are increasingly challenging the state itself and the Hosni Mubarak regime, which the United States has long supported as a bastion of stability and moderation in the region.

One conclusion that could be drawn from this is the need, for analytic and policy purposes, to distinguish between radical Islam, which is implacably hostile to the West, and more moderate Islam, with which we can probably have good relations. A second conclusion is that the old corporatist system of controls on civil society is being increasingly challenged and transformed, at least in the more advanced countries. But still a third conclusion is that Egyptian (and other Middle Eastern) civil society is moving from corporatism to Islamicism, and that neither is particularly liberal-democratic or in accord with the Western idea of civil society.

As the Islamic challenge to the Egyptian state has grown, the state itself has tended to become more repressive. The pattern sounds like that of Latin America in the 1960s and 1970s when a wave of military authoritarianism swept that area. Egypt has become more and more a police state. Mubarak stays in power in large part because the army and police keep him there. The National Assembly is largely a rubber stamp and elections are manipulated. The press is censored and the mass media controlled by the Information Ministry. Civil society and opposition groups are increasingly repressed. As the Islamist groups grow in strength, so does the government's willingness to violate civil liberties and use force against them. Democracy is increasingly seen as a sham; civil society is either being eliminated, suppressed, or taking intolerant directions.[14]

In looking at Egypt and the Middle East, one is reminded more of South Africa and the "bureaucratic authoritarianism" of Latin America of past decades than of recent successful civil society development and democratization. First, civil society is more often in decline than it is growing. Second, when it does emerge, it takes a form—corporatist, now increasingly Islamicist—that is not liberal, pluralist, tolerant, or democratic. Third, the state is inclined to use repression against it; meanwhile, the state itself may be disintegrating. It is not a pretty picture for those who favor democratic pluralism and a tolerant, autonomous, free-wheeling, dynamic, competitive civil society.

THE INTERNATIONAL CONTEXT

For the last quarter-century, and particularly since President Anwar Sadat's 1979 decision to support the Middle Eastern peace process, Egypt has been the recipient of a mammoth international—mainly U.S.—foreign aid program. Now totaling over $52 billion, the amount of foreign aid given to Egypt is second only to that given Israel. The aid is mainly designed to ensure that peace endures at least from the Egyptian side and to demonstrate to the Egyptian public that avoiding war would improve their lives.[15]

The assistance is multipurpose, with much of it going to military equipment and training. On the civilian side, the aid has gone to a variety of developmental panaceas that have come and gone over the years, including family planning, basic human needs, sustainable development, and, most recently, civil society. Overall, one could say that the project has been successful in terms of its basic objectives: Egypt has not gone to war with Israel in recent decades; Mubarak has been a generally moderate voice in the Middle East; and Egyptian per-capita income has slowly inched up from about $1,000 per year to approximately $1,500.

U.S. AID has done a lot of long-term development projects in Egypt: schools, roads, agriculture, water resources, even mosques. By common consensus and keeping in mind the long term, a number of these programs have been successful. U.S. assistance has also sought to improve the performance of Egypt's governmental institutions: the courts, customs, tax collection, bureaucratic performance, etc.

U.S. AID has tried to instigate privatization, anti-corruption, and programs that reduce the size of the state, but the verdict is not yet in on most of these latter programs.

The aid program has also begun to focus on developing Egyptian civil society, but in this area the results have been even less successful. Without here going into the details of these programs, the "big picture" offers abundant reasons to be skeptical. First, Egypt is an authoritarian regime so that the programs to improve elections, build political parties, and develop genuinely competitive democracy are seldom looked on with favor by the government. Second, when there is a clash between the security (Middle East peace) and the democratizing aspects of U.S. policy, the security argument always trumps all others, often to the detriment of democracy. Third, as civil society began to emerge in Egypt, it was usually co-opted by the government and organized in a corporatist fashion rather than a liberal-pluralist one. And fourth, if and when the foreign aid programs supported oppositionist "civil society" groups as a way, presumably, of building or strengthening democracy and pluralism, it ran up against the uncomfortable fact that most of these groups were Islamicist incorporating varying degrees of fundamentalism—not exactly what the United States wants to support. Moreover, a double negative whammy: supporting oppositionist groups might undermine the overall policy goal of securing a stable, peaceful Egypt; it might also strengthen the fundamentalists whose commitment to democracy is suspect and to whose policy goals many Americans object.

The policy mantra from most U.S. officials, journalists, and scholars who know the Middle East is as follows: (1) rising Islamic fundamentalism is a fact of life; (2) we need to deal with that fact realistically and not just ignore it or wish it away; (3) not all fundamentalist movements are the same nor are all of them anti-American and a threat to us; (4) the United States, therefore, needs to get on the side of history by distinguishing between the violent and anti-American Islamic fundamentalist groups who want to create an Iran-like theocratic state or who support Osama bin Laden–like terrorism, *and* the more moderate, usually middle-class business and professional groups whose aims of religious revival and national modernization we can live with and even support.

But such a policy is fraught with difficulties: first, most Americans—including many public officials—do not acknowledge or recognize such a sharp distinction between the various Islamic fundamentalist groups; second, the policy runs up against the dilemma that U.S. policy in the Middle East is dominated by strategic considerations (peace, oil, Israel, stability) and less so by a democracy/civil society agenda; third, the Congress and the U.S. government generally have trouble dealing with admittedly authoritarian regimes that are not very democratic and often violate human rights. Fourth, the United States tends not to understand well or empathize with Islamic societies and peoples, which may be enough to discourage major new initiatives in the area; fifth, in a context of scarce foreign aid resources or attention to foreign affairs, attention to Middle Eastern civil society is not high on the list of priorities; and sixth, many Americans have concluded that Islam and democracy/civil society are incompatible so we should not put many resources into a hopeless situation.

CONCLUSION

There is considerable attention and ferment in the Middle East with regard to the concept of civil society. For one thing, the traditional civil society of the tribe, the clan, the bazaar is beginning to give way—to be replaced or supplemented by what? For another, new groups organized around new concepts such as the environment or human rights are beginning to organize. Third, new social movements of workers, women, and students are mobilizing in the Middle East, groups that have for a long time been organized under statist-corporatist auspices but are now pointing toward greater autonomy. Fourth, there is the phenomenon of Islamic fundamentalism and its place in "civil society"; alternatively, how does this new phenomenon of civil society fit or apply in an Islamic setting? And fifth, civil society has by now acquired a certain international cachet that makes it worthy of attention in this area not heretofore known for the strength of civil society.

But in the Middle East the precise meaning and implications of civil society are still ambiguous. In Iran, for example, civil society has come to mean the "rule of law" and the "rule of the people"—not necessarily pluralism or countervailing interest groups as in the Western conception. In other countries "civil society" is used to advocate honest elections, greater power to the parliament, regional or ethnic group autonomy from the central state, or as a cover for oppositionist politics, including terrorism. Civil society groups in many of the area's autocratic regimes are often limited to such issues as the environment—issues that can be dealt with without (unlike opposition or human rights groups) threatening the regime in power. Some of my interviewees in the Middle East now use the term GNGOs (governmental-nongovernmental organizations), a contradiction in terms to American civil society advocates whose definition requires that civil society groups *not* be governmental, and that sounds like a new, more socially acceptable term for corporatism. In addition, in a variety of countries, opposition groups are now organizing as "study groups" or "civic movements," using the umbrella of "civil society," to disguise or "front" for their potentially destabilizing political activities. The concept of "civil society" by now carries so many meanings, gradations, and implications that the concept may have lost all precise meaning.

That many of these more-or-less autonomous organizations exist is certain; so is the fact of considerable attention to and ferment regarding civil society. Far less certain, however, is the viability of all these groups and their commitment to democracy. For one thing, civil society in the Middle East is still weak by Western standards. Second, it is often used and abused by regimes in power to put in place corporatist or GNGO (!) systems that have little or no autonomy from the state. Third, as civil society has emerged, the strongest groups have frequently been those based on Islamic fundamental-ism—not in accord with most Americans' conception of civil soci-ety. And fourth, there seems to be no correlation, so far, between the rise of civil society (by whatever definition) in the Middle East *and* democracy. Indeed, as Kamrava and Mora conclude, "if the latest democratic wave has been on a global march since the early to mid-1980s, it has either completely skipped the Middle East or has yet to make its introduction to the area."[16]

NOTES

1. The issues are posed in *The Civil Society Debate in Middle Eastern Stud-ies*, Near East Center Colloquium Series, with contributions by James Gelvin, Augustus Norton, Roger Gwen, and Diane Singerman.

2. Anwar H. Syed, "Islamic Models of Development," in Howard J. Wiarda (ed.), *Non-Western Theories of Development* (Fort Worth: Harcourt Brace, 1999), pp. 99–115.

3. Anwar Syed, "Democracy and Islam: Are They Compatible?" in Howard J. Wiarda (ed.), *Comparative Democracy and Democratization* (Fort Worth: Harcourt Brace, 2001), pp. 127–43.

4. Mahmood Monshipouri, "Islamism, Civil Society, and the Democracy Conundrum," *The Muslim World*, 57 (January 1997), 54–66.

5. Debbie Lovatt, "Islam, Secularism, and Civil Society," *The World Today* (August/September 1997), 226–28.

6. Mehran Kamrava and Frank O. Mora, "Civil Society and Democratiza-tion in Comparative Perspective: Latin America and the Middle East," *Third World Quarterly*, 19, 5 (1998), 893–915.

7. Louis Cantori, "Civil Society, Liberalism, and the Corporatist Alterna-tive in the Middle East," *Middle East Studies Association Bulletin*, 31, 1 (1997).

8. Robert Bianchi, *Unruly Corporatism: Associational Life in Twentieth Century Egypt* (New York: Oxford University Press, 1989).

9. Kamrava and Mora, "Civil Society and Democratization," pp. 894–95.

10. David Collier and Ruth Berins Collier, *Shaping the Political Arena: Critical Junctures, the Labor Movement, and Regime Dynamics in Latin*

America (Princeton: Princeton University Press, 1991). This book has implications beyond its geographic focus.

11. Cantori, "Civil Society," p. 38.

12. Marsha Pripstein Posusney, *Labor and the State in Egypt* (New York: Columbia University Press, 1997).

13. Geneive Abdo, "How Moderate Islam Is Transforming Egypt," *The Washington Post* (November 5, 2000), p. B5; Diane Singerman, "Civil Society in the Shadow of the Egyptian State: The Role of Informal Networks in the Construction of Public Life," in Norton (ed.), *The Civil Society Debate*.

14. Thomas Cromwell, "Egypt Is a Police State," *International Herald Tribune* (May 29, 2001), p. 9.

15. *The Washington Post* (December 26, 2000), p. A1.

16. Kamrava and Mora, "Civil Society and Democratization," p. 893.

Part IV

CONCLUSION

8

IS CIVIL
SOCIETY EXPORTABLE?

*The American Model
and Third World Development*

This conclusion is divided into four parts. The first part summarizes in general terms the main themes, issues, and controversies surrounding the civil society debate, why the concept is so attractive but also why we need to be careful in its use. The second part reviews in comparative terms what common patterns emerge from the case studies included in the book. The third part contains a general critique of "civil society" viewed as a magic "cure-all" or panacea for the ills of the developing nations. The fourth part offers some constructive guidelines for NGOs and policy makers working on civil society development.

SUMMARY

Civil society has become a topic of increasing interest in recent years. Scholars have examined its historic theoretical and philosophic foundations; the U.S. government has built civil society requirements into many of its foreign aid programs as well as overall foreign policy; and, rather like Lana Turner in a tight sweater waiting to be "discovered" in the proverbial drugstore on Hollywood and Vine, the foundations and international lending agencies have settled on civil society as their latest "discovery" to solve the problems of the world. Many nongovernmental organizations (NGOs) are similarly integrating civil society concepts into their programs; civil society is being touted by the Third World as holding great promise for assisting democratization and national development efforts; still others see civil society grandiosely as "saving the world."[1]

One can readily understand why the notion of civil society is so attractive, particularly to scholars, foundations, policy advocates, and the NGO community. First, it has a nice ring to it: civil society as a term sounds lofty, nonpartisan, citizen-oriented, participatory, and democratic; and who could argue with those attributes? Second, civil society conjures up images of Madisonian, Tocquevillian pluralism, town meetings, grassroots participation, checks and balances, and countervailing yet ultimately harmonious interest-group competition and democratic public policy. The images most of us have of civil society include bowling leagues, PTAs, soccer moms, girl and boy scouts, neighborhood associations, town meetings, and peaceful, harmonious collective bargaining.[2] All of these conjure up favorable images to the American Congress, public, and policy makers.

A third reason why civil society is so attractive is that it holds promise of taking policy making out of the hands of often corrupt, venal bureaucracies, governments, and "evil" international organizations like the WTO or the IMF, and placing it directly in the hands of popular organizations, or "the people." Fourth (and this by no means exhausts the list), civil society is popular because it looks "just like us" or at least what we imagine ourselves to be: democratic, grassroots-oriented, participatory, pluralist. It seems as a concept to avoid all of America's bad attributes (the influence of money on politics, gridlock between the executive and legislative branches, large, impersonal bureaucracy, and so on) and to restore an earlier, more pristine form of citizen participation, interest-group balance, and direct democracy. Civil society has thus taken on aspects of a civic renewal, the apparent rediscovery of our long-lost and better attributes, even in some quarters a quasi-religious crusade and re-conversion.[3]

Over the last two decades policy makers have also recognized the importance of civil society and have seized upon it as an instrument of foreign policy. For example, in the 1980s and 1990s the United States government and others used emerging civil society organizations to assist in the ouster of discredited authoritarian regimes (Marcos, Duvalier, etc.) as well as, through Solidarity and other organizations, in the overthrow of communist regimes in Eastern Europe. Recognizing the incapacity and/or corruption of central governments, civil society organizations have been used to carry out policies in the areas of family planning, education, environmentalism, and democratization. Civil society has proved a means to "think globally but act locally" on a variety of policy fronts; civil society has also proved to be a useful conduit for U.S. and other foreign assistance programs. Where civil society has not existed in many Third World nations, the United States, including the government, AID, foundations, and American civil society groups, has created, aided, and even invented it, obviously for its own national interest purposes as well as because we believe it assists democracy in the Third World. Already in these comments we can find several reasons to begin to worry about the civil society approach.

This last aspect raises a familiar Washington issue. Whenever a concept like civil society has so many positives, achieves widespread popularity and consensus, and seems to accomplish so many positive goals (overthrowing both authoritarianism and communism) at once, its attractiveness to politicians becomes irresistible. The concept then becomes politicized and is used for purposes other than those intended. Already AID, the State Department, the Defense Department, the CIA, the White House, Congress, and sundry others have latched onto the concept. In addition, the National Endowment for Democracy, the Republican and Democratic international affairs institutes, the Ford and MacArthur Foundations, the Washington think tanks, and numerous human rights and religious groups have similarly seized on the concept. "Civil society" has become a growth industry. And when that happens, the concept itself and its purposes run the risk of being hopelessly distorted. It also runs the risk of falling victim to the same policy cycle that so many other well-meaning programs in the past—agrarian reform, community development, family planning, basic human needs, sustainable development—have gone through: initial excitement and enthusiasm, followed by politicization and distortion, resulting in disillusionment, disappointment, and eventual petering out (but never complete *disappearance*; remember, these are *government* and *bureaucratic* programs). My reading is that civil society, parallel to these other panaceas, has now about exhausted its romantic and enthusiastic phase and is presently on the cusp of either decline or a more realistic assessment.

The issues are compounded once the concept travels abroad. First, as we have seen, different societies and cultures mean different things by civil society than do Lockean, Tocquevillian, Madisonian Americans. Second, the *form* that civil society takes in different countries may vary greatly from the U.S. model—and not all of these by any means are liberal, pluralist, and democratic. Third, there is money involved—now often big money—and there are legions of opportunists in the United States and abroad waiting to take advantage of the largesse now going into civil society projects. Often these are the same opportunists who had earlier milked other AID and U.S. government panaceas—agrarian reform, community development, etc.—dry, without producing much in the way of reform. And fourth, when host governments observe civil society activities, which by their nature are often oppositionist, outside of state control, and liberal-pluralist in the U.S. mold, the temptation is powerful to control, regulate, co-opt, and expel, or repress them. Elites and national governments in Latin America, East Asia, and elsewhere have used, and continue to use, *corporatism* as a way to harness and control pluralist interest groups;[4] now, since corporatism at the national level is being gradually replaced in many countries by at least the forms of neoliberalism, it is being resurrected at the local level where civil society groups are increasingly being required to register, divulge their members' names, disclose their financing, and seek recognition or "juridical personality" from local authorities, which also carries with it the possibility of nonrecognition and, therefore, suppression if the group persists in its activities.

When the idea for this research project on comparative civil society was first proposed, its thrust was aimed at suggesting ways to dismantle the corporatist structures we have found so prevalent in the various Third World areas studied, and to move quickly toward democratic, genuinely pluralist civil society. Those remain the long-term objectives. But in the course of the research it became plain that dismantling corporatist controls over interest-group activities too quickly or precipitously would in most countries produce instability and possibly chaos and disintegration. The research instead suggests that corporatism ought to be seen as a transitional regime between authoritarianism and democracy. As in South Korea, Taiwan, Brazil, Mexico, and hopefully Egypt, corporatism in its more benign forms should be viewed as a way of gradually bridging the transition to democracy and civil society but without producing ungovernability and breakdown. Most countries need to e. . . a. . . s. . . e their way to democracy and civil society, to establish a solid socioeconomic foundation, and then to gradually let up on the controls. Rather than dismantling corporatism, therefore, in most Third World countries it needs to be viewed as an intermediary stage on the road to democracy and pluralism, the delicate balance of which requires deft handling, mainly by officials and politicians within these countries who know their own often delicate political situations better than the American or international officials advising them.

These preliminary conclusions suggest the need for caution in our enthusiasm for civil society. What began as a noble and ennobling concept seems to go through, as with the other policy panaceas previously noted, a familiar life cycle: initial popularity and enthusiasm, widespread acceptance, then politicization, distortion, and decline. I judge that civil society is just now on the verge of these more realistic but otherwise disillusioning, downward-sloping transformations. Hence, a cautious and prudent approach to civil society rather than an excessively enthusiastic one may be called for.

Patterns from the Case Studies

The case studies contained in this book stand by themselves with their own conclusions; what may be even more useful to the reader at this stage is the *general patterns* that emerge from the cases presented.

The first conclusion is that in all the countries/areas studied, there has been over the last twenty to thirty years an impressive growth in the number and density of civil society and that, on balance, this has been good for the establishment and spread of democracy and pluralism.

Second, the case studies reveal tremendous variety in the kinds, types, priorities, cultural and philosophical bases, developmental levels, and systems of civil society and of state-society relations. History, culture, religion, as well as levels of socioeconomic development were all important factors in explaining the varieties of civil society. No one size fits all, nor are all civil society organizations automatically, universally, or by definition beneficial for democracy, stability, and pluralism. More on this below.

Third, civil society growth has been general and universal but it received particular stimulus during times of crisis or challenge: the struggle for democracy in Latin America, the anti-authoritarianism movements in Asia, the anti-apartheid struggle in South Africa, and the struggle for freedom and democracy in Eastern Europe. It is usually the case that, since other groups (political parties and the like) are proscribed, oppositionist civil society constituted the only or main opposition to dictatorial rule, and it attracted widespread support.

Fourth, in the early stages of the emergence of civil society, foreign support and finances are often crucial. Foreign donors and aid agencies are not only critical in assisting civil society, however, but often they literally create civil society to serve their own foreign policy goals as well as those of the local society, and therein lies a major problem.

Fifth, once that early crisis or challenge had been met and the goal (democracy, freedom, the end of apartheid) accomplished, civil society growth tends to drop off precipitously. The issue fades, international donors and supporters lose interest, the leaders and many members of the formerly opposition groups get patronage jobs in the new government, and the previously proscribed political parties and more institutionalized interest groups reassert themselves and often take over the agendas and followers of the earlier civil society movements.

Sixth, there are clear correlations between political culture and civil society: the United States and other nations that are products of British institutions and political culture tend to have strong societies and weak states; in contrast, Asian, Latin American, and African societies tend to have, at least by aspiration, strong state systems but weak civil society. Civil society in Islamic states tends to be weaker still or almost nonexistent.

There is also a correlation, seventh, between civil society and levels of socioeconomic development: countries that are more developed socially and economically tend to have stronger, more robust civil societies.

Eighth, there appears to be a class bias in civil society development: in the early stages a number of lower-class or mass movements are mobilized; at later stages, middle-class and elite elements tend to dominate civil society.

Often parallel with this last development, ninth, comes a tendency for state reassertion of limits, controls, and co-optation of civil society groups. In other words, corporatism, now of a more open kind, tends to reassert itself, often at the expense of free associability.

Nevertheless, tenth, even with the reassertion of corporatism, there tends to be a considerably greater level of freedom, pluralism, and openness than under the earlier authoritarian regime. Corporatism and pluralism, statism and free associability, may *both* be present, coexisting in an often uneasy but always dynamic relationship.

Eleventh, what one finds at present is an incredible mix of civil society groups: some genuinely autonomous from the state and supporting democracy and human rights, others manifestly hostile to these goals, still others co-opted and controlled corporatist-style by the state, as well as new, complex public-private or state-society partnerships.

Twenty Reasons to
Be Skeptical of Civil Society

While the idea of civil society has a nice ring and reputation, its practice in the Third World, and particularly the efforts of the U.S. government as well as NGOs to export it abroad, have produced decidedly mixed results. Here we report on the numerous problems in seeking to export civil society; in the last section of the chapter we return to more hopeful themes and seek to assess what we should do, or not do, in promoting civil society.

(1) Civil Society as Panacea

Over the decades since we first started to pay attention to the developing world, American foreign aid and the international donor community have settled on a variety of "solutions" to Third World problems that later on prove to have been panaceas. The list of these panaceas is familiar to anyone with experience in foreign aid programs since the 1960s: the Alliance for Progress, infrastructure development, agrarian reform, community development, family planning, basic human needs, sustainable development, now civil society. Typically these programs begin with great hope and fanfare, are well-funded for a time, then run into the harsh realities of politics and social structure in Third World countries or the fleeting, fickle interest of the American public and Congress, prove less successful than expected, start to run downhill, are effectively abandoned but are never quite dismantled because whole networks of bureaucratic and private interests grow up around them, and eventually are replaced by a new panacea. Is "civil society" about to go through the same life cycle? My own sense is that it is, that it currently, as a relatively fresh new idea, still has *cachet* with the Congress, foundations, intellectuals, and activists; but that the first serious studies are starting to come in with disappointing results, and that, therefore, this concept will soon (may have already) begun its downward slide as have so many of these other cure-alls in the past.[5]

(2) Theory Versus Reality

Civil society sounds wonderful in the abstract: democratic, pluralist, private sector-oriented, Tocquevillian, nonbureaucratic, Madisonian, participatory, like a New England town meeting full of yeoman citizens. The reality, however, is often considerably less than that. In practice in too many countries, "civil society" has been conceived in statist and corporatist terms, as a way to siphon money out of international donors without providing much in the way of reform, as a facade for authoritarian practices, as a way to control and limit new social and political groups rather than as an avenue for genuine democratization. Egypt is a case in point—greater authoritarianism rather than less—but there are many others.

(3) Risks and Benefits

Civil society is undoubtedly beneficial where it works. But suppose, as in Indonesia and possibly India, the growth of civil society and the pluralism it engenders weaken governmental authority and policy making in countries where the state's ability to deliver public services is already too weak? Or it leads to the breakup of the state, with disastrous, disintegrative, anarchic consequences? Suppose civil society emerges as a substitute for and, therefore, weakens political parties, which most analysts believe to be absolutely essential for democracy? Suppose civil society undermines traditional but time-tested modes of interest articulation and aggregation (tribes, clientelist relations, caste associations, ethnic coteries), leaving societies with the worst of all possible worlds: old interest associations undermined before the newer civil society ones have had a chance to take root.

(4) Varieties of Civil Society

Most of us know what we have in mind by civil society: liberal, pluralist, Tocquevillian, democratic, participatory. But our theoretical survey has highlighted the variety of conceptions of civil society: totalitarian, authoritarian, corporatist, Rousseauian, Lockean. Only the last conforms to our preferred liberal model. In the developing world the most prevalent form is still corporatist (state-regulated, officially controlled), with some preference for the Rousseauian solution (direct rule, no intermediaries) combined (often under foreign pressure) with some, usually grudging acquiescence in the Lockean-Madisonian model. In addition, there are Confucian, Buddhist, Islamic, and a variety of non-Western and indigenous forms of civil society, and various mixes and overlaps of these with the Western imports. The variety of outcomes should give us pause before we too precipitously pursue the civil society route. And in many countries liberal, corporatist, non-democratic, and separatist forms of civil society exist simultaneously in a potentially potent, explosive, disintegrative mix.

(5) Nondemocratic Civil Society: A Diversity of "Civil Society" Conceptions

The above point is so crucial that it deserves reiteration in another framework. Civil society development will not necessarily, inevitably, or universally lead to more democratic, liberal, or socially just outcomes. At least equally plausible are authoritarian, statist, corporatist, and Rousseauian outcomes. To say nothing of nondemocratic Islamic, Confucian, ethnic, clientelistic outcomes. Even more likely are mixed or combined systems in which elites and those in power maneuver and manipulate to satisfy diverse constituencies, allowing just enough civil society to keep international donors and domestic social groups satisfied, but not so much that the elites' own power and position are threatened.

The research points to the conclusion that this is one of the key problems of the effort to export civil society. My interviews reveal that almost all of the American government and NGO officials involved in promoting civil society abroad have in mind a very narrow, parochial, and particular notion of civil society based on the U.S. experience. That is, naturally enough, the Lockean, Madisonian, Tocquevillian, and very American concept of civil society with which we are all familiar because it is part of the American tradition in which we all grew up. But when it is suggested that we need to be familiar also with Confucian, Islamic, clientelistic, Rousseauian, corporatist, and other "strange" forms of civil society, American officials are often completely lost. They cannot conceive of a form of civil society other than our own American version. So when faced with non-Western or various mixed forms, they do not know what to do other than falling back on the American model, which may be inappropriate in various Third World settings, and blaming the country involved for not living up to the American-style system we have designed for them or for not moving fast enough toward the desired goal. This is not only a response certain to produce failure and frustration on the part of all parties (U.S. *and* host country officials) but also to run the risk of damaging and destabilizing the very countries we are seeking to assist.

(6) Limited Pluralism; Ambiguity and Different Meanings in the Term "Civil Society"

As Latin America, Asia, and other Third World areas have developed, new social and political groups have emerged, including business and commercial elements, a larger middle class, trade unions, women, peasants, indigenous elements, and others. But in most of these countries this is still often limited, controlled, regulated pluralism, not the unfettered, free-wheeling, unregulated, virtually anarchic pluralism of U.S. political society. Even in newly democratic regimes, civil society groups still must often be recognized, legitimated, and licensed by the state, which, of course, is not very democratic. Nor does most of the developing world practice the kind of pluralist interest-group lobbying found in the United States. So while we applaud the ofttimes greater pluralism of these societies, we still need to recognize that there are degrees and gradations of pluralism, that some groups are better organized and more influential than others, and that some, often very large social sectors, are not organized or represented at all.

The above paragraph emphasizes a key problem: the ambiguity and the many distinct meanings in the concept of civil society. Americans are in agreement, à la Madison, Tocqueville, and interest-group pluralism, that it means a web of associational life autonomous from the state and intermediary between the state and the family or individual, groups competing vigorously in the public sphere. But other societies mean something quite different by the term. In this study we have seen definitions that range from "the rule of law," "competitive elections," "separation of powers," to "tribalism," "ethnic identity," "clientelism," and many others. So when we talk about "civil society," Americans and the rest of the world are often talking about quite different meanings, concepts, and understandings. Other cultures also give civil society a different—and usually lesser—priority than do Americans. A final and critical point is that most other societies see a greater role for state regulation of interest-group activity than do Americans and do not see such an overriding need for "autonomy from the state" as in the U.S. definition. Clearly, given these differences, it will be hard to arrive at a common understanding of civil society, let alone a common policy agenda to promote such a vague, ambiguous concept.

(7) Biases of Civil Society
There are many biases in the civil society literature and in the actions of civil society groups; here we enumerate only a few of them. First, the foreign foundations, donor groups, and strongest apostles of civil society are overwhelmingly liberal, activist, and associated with the U.S. Democratic Party, although Republicans may support the concept as well. There is of course nothing wrong with partisanship as long as we recognize that's what it is. Second, the movements abroad that these groups support tend not only to be similarly liberal, often radical, activist, and on the left, but also, almost by the definition of civil society itself, oppositionist and anti-government. To be identified with such anti-government activism, which may or may not be justified and is usually some fuzzy combination of the two, is very dangerous for outside groups and may lead to suppression, suspension of program activities, expulsion, and, overall, the over-politicization of program activities. A third bias is the actions of these outside groups, often naive and well-meaning but sometimes destructive as well, when they get involved in the internal affairs of other nations. A dramatic case in point is in the Mexican state of Chiapas, where many foreign NGOs have identified with and aided the revolutionary *Zapatista* movement; the

Mexican government has sought to regulate and control them in classic corporatist fashion (hard to do with foreign-based groups while undergoing democratization and liberalization, and under media scrutiny at the same time), and finally threw up its hands in disgust and expelled many of the organizations from the country. This is not a forward step for civil society. There are *numerous* instances of foreign NGOs or the U.S. government using local, almost always U.S.-financed groups, to intervene in the internal affairs of other nations, and almost always as a way to influence political events in these countries.[6]

(8) Whom to Include
Most of us have a conception of civil society that includes peasant groups, labor unions, women's groups, maybe political parties, neighborhood and community groups, human rights organizations, and—above all—bowling leagues![7] But if we define civil society, as we must, as *all* those associations that are intermediary between state and citizen, we may have to include business groups, oligarchic sectors, paramilitaries, guerrillas, drug barons, and certainly in Latin America the Roman Catholic Church (historically more than a "mere" interest group, part of the state structure) as well as the rising Pentecostal movements. Now let us complicate the issue even more by including such unlovable groups as the European skinheads and the North American militias or the Ku Klux Klan, South African racists, terroristic Islamic fundamentalists, and violent and separatist ethnic movements.

An even more complex issue is presented by African ethnicity and tribalism, Indian caste associations, and Latin American patronage networks. Each of these is "parochial" and "traditional" in some senses, and we would probably prefer in terms of promoting modernization to confine them to the dustbins of history. Yet African tribalism often provides the only public and social services that many communities have; India's caste associations have become rather like modern interest associations and political parties; and without patronage networks to "grease" the machinery of government much of Latin America, the Middle Eastern states, Africa, and Southeast Asia (plus Louisiana, Arkansas, and a few other states) would collapse. In short, there are a large variety of civil society groups including many that we don't particularly like politically or consider passé or that are violent, destructive, and hateful. On the other hand, civil society has to be viewed as like democracy: if that is what you want, then you have to be prepared to accept the outcome of the process even if it produces results in the form of groups that you may find abhorrent.

(9) Weakened States?

The concept of civil society implies limits on state authority; indeed, that is its purpose: to develop intermediaries between the state and its citizens that rein in the potential for the exercise of dictatorial power. However, the problem in many developing countries is no longer excessive state power (as it was in the 1970s under authoritarianism) but a state that, like other institutions in society and civil society itself, is weak, underdeveloped, and thus ineffective. Many Third World states, ostensibly strong and powerful, cannot make their writ felt in remote areas and are ineffective in carrying out the policies most of us would approve.[8] The problem in these societies may not be a too-strong state and, therefore, the need for the mediating influence and checks and balances of civil society, but a too-weak state that cannot govern or carry out effective public policies. Alternatively, the growth of civil society in ethnically divided (Indonesia) or fragmented (Argentina) societies may lead not to democracy but to divisions, ungovernability, and breakdown. My own view is the balanced one that we need both a strong and effective civil society and a strong and effective state, but with the current emphasis almost entirely on civil society we run the risks of rendering states powerless and thus contributing to further fragmentation and ungovernability, already a major problem in many Third World nations.

A related issue involves the possible *reassertion* of state authority under threat of new challenges and provocations. We should not view the growth of civil society as necessarily inevitable, universal, irreversible, or as a result of inexorable development—although in the relatively peaceful 1980s and 1990s it might have appeared that way.

From the perspective of post–September 11, 2001, and the terrorist at-
tacks launched against the United States and other countries, many
governments, threatened by ethnic, separatist, Islamic fundamentalist,
terrorist, and disintegrative forces, are reversing past trends and
strengthening statist and coercive forces. In the process, many civil
society groups are being disbanded, harassed, and broken up, or having new restrictions placed on their activities. So while in the short
run strengthened civil society seemed to be leading to weaker, less authoritarian, more democratic states, in the new circumstances we may
be seeing a weakening of civil society and the corresponding strengthening of state structures, including reimposed authoritarian controls.

(10) Ethnocentrism
Much of the literature on civil society seems to be based on the
perception that one model fits all. And that one model, not sur-
prising since that is where the modern version of the concept orig-
inated, almost always bears a striking resemblance to the Lockean,
Madisonian, Tocquevillian, Hartzian liberalism and interest-group
pluralism of the United States. But we have already seen that there
are different models of civil society and state-society relations in the
West; when we get to the non-West the differences become even
more striking. Japan, South Korea, and Taiwan are all democracies
and developed nations but with only weak civil society; the Islamic
world similarly has weak civil society but almost no democracy at
all. It seems to me the height of arrogance and ethnocentrism for
the United States to proclaim that one size fits all, especially when
that one size is modeled on ourselves and our own often *particular*
history and society. Such a perception will in any case not work; we
cannot export our model to societies where it does not fit and where
the history, economy, sociology, and political culture are so much
different from our own.[9] Meanwhile, Japan and quite a number of
other nations seem to be doing quite well economically and as
democracies without having a strong civil society. Civil society may,
therefore, not be the critical variable in either democracy or development that is often suggested.

(11) Sharks and Opportunists

In both the donor countries and the developing recipient ones, there are sharks and opportunists waiting to pounce on the latest program emanating from Washington and turn it to their own private financial or political advantage. I have been following the life cycles of these various programs since the beginning of the Alliance for Progress in the early 1960s, and it is striking how often the same people, whether on the U.S. contractor or consultant end or the developing country recipient end, are consistently involved. This cannot be sheer coincidence, nor is it simply that the same people will consistently have an interest in parallel progressive policies. In the developing countries that I know best, whether the issue is agrarian reform, community development, basic human needs, family planning, sustainable development, and now civil society, the same people always seem to form the local commissions and agencies that show the aid donors how and where to spend their monies. It is not merely love of public policy issues that motivates these persons; having been in quite a number of their homes, I can report that, as in political Washington, they have learned to "do well by doing good"; that is, by profiting personally and/or politically by jumping quickly on the bandwagon of every new U.S. initiative that comes down the pike. Indeed, quite a few of these individuals are widely admired in their own countries on nationalistic grounds for having, over a forty-year period, milked and hoodwinked the (usually) American donor agencies while enriching themselves and rising to positions of prominence in the process. Of course, most of us will respond that "*my* friends and contacts would never do that and in any case there are controls in place"; but my experience is that the locals are at least as practiced as the donors at political machinations and are adept at taking advantage of these programs for private gain.

(12) A Weak Popular Base?

The figures we have for all of Latin America indicate that only 13 percent of the population are members of civil society in any form; for other areas the numbers are even smaller. This figure includes political party, labor group, peasant group, women's group, community group, religious and other group members of all kinds. First, this is an incredibly low density number as compared with Western Europe or North America and offers scant evidence for the prospect of a mushrooming civil society in Latin America—or elsewhere in the developing world—anytime in the near future. Second, persons in Latin America tend heavily to be members of one group and one group only; one does not find the webs of multiple and crosscutting group memberships that one finds in U.S. society that tend to moderate the citizen's position on any one issue. Rather, in Latin America one tends to go "all out" for the singular group of which one is a member, thus producing a society of almost stock types—*the* oligarch, *the* cleric, *the* military officer, *the* unionist, *the* student, etc.—whose behavior must conform to the stereotype. Such stereotyping and the rigidities of the categories, which probably go back to the social hierarchies of Saint Thomas, are not supportive of the moderating and stabilizing tendencies that civil society is supposed to engender.[10] Third, "civil society" in *all* of the areas investigated, particularly after the more immediate crisis (e.g., the struggle for a democratic election) has passed, is usually limited to elite and upper-middle-class groups, while the organization of the mass population is usually weak and inchoate.

(13) A Product of Political Leaders and Intellectuals?
"Civil society" now has a certain *cachet*. Everyone among *our* friends and colleagues seems to agree it's a good thing. But are these sentiments widespread or are they only the preferences of government officials, party leaders, bureaucrats, and intellectuals? Has anyone yet checked with the mass of the populations of the developing world to see if they believe in civil society as much as we do? The few survey results we have indicate that, when it is explained to them, people often have a favorable view of civil society; at the same time, it remains vague, distant, and divorced from everyday realities. At the local level, people may be reluctant to get involved; traditional fatalism is still widespread; and in those many countries based on the Napoleonic

Code, one waits for guidance and direction from the central ministries, not relying on grassroots mobilization at the base. The issue may be parallel to that of "sustainable development," a concept to which the Brazilian government with considerable reluctance eventually agreed; meanwhile, Brazilian peasants, often with that same government's approval, continued to cut, burn, and "pave over" the Amazon basin, which supplies 40 percent of the world's oxygen. So with "civil society": government and political leaders and intellectuals approve at least in the abstract, but meantime overriding material interest and self-preservation often take priority.

(14) Divorced from Power Realities?
Civil society cannot be seen as some magic formula that, as the title of a recent conference puts it, will "save the world." Instead, civil society must be seen in a broader political and power configuration. No government is going to favor civil society if in the process it sees its own power base eroding by the mobilization of new social sectors. Instead, it will try to co-opt, control, regulate, and maybe even repress civil society, to offer carrots or sticks or maybe both at once. At the same time, civil society groups will try to mobilize international public opinion and support to maintain their autonomy and freedom of action. These are political processes that will produce multiple outcomes and a mixed bag of results.

Let us take Mexico, whose complexities we can only barely begin to unpack here. On the one hand, there is the official or state-run corporate structure of civil society (organized labor, business, farmers, professional associations), whose leaders in the face of a disintegrating state system and an opposition electoral victory are frantically scrambling to renegotiate their relationship with the state, the official Revolutionary Institutional Party (PRI), and the new government. On the other hand, there is the new, freer civil society widely credited with helping Mexico democratize over the last thirty years and now entering into a new relationship with the government and the citizens. These respective groups are renegotiating their relations not only with the state but also with each other, where conflict between the official labor, peasant, Indian, and business groups and the independent or civil society ones is intense and sometimes violent. Within these conglomerates of groups, negotiations and political relations are proceeding at different speeds; and in the south of Mexico the *Zapatistas* and other "civil society" groups have opted out of the co-optation game to pursue a radical agenda and guerrilla tactics. They are opposed by both the regular armed forces and police and by paramilitaries—another unlovely but often effective civil society group. Meanwhile, there are a host of foreign or foreign-sponsored groups whose relations with the government are complicated precisely because they are often nonnational. I count at least six state-civil society arenas here with multiple possible outcomes. To me this is all political process and interest politics with only limited relations to some idealistic goal of advancing civil society.[11]

(15) Outside Sponsorship and Control

A related problem is that of outside, or foreign, sponsorship, control, and manipulation of civil society groups. In the Dominican Republic, for example, the U.S. Embassy had concluded that the aging and increasingly infirm President Joaquín Balaguer was not only corrupt but that his continuation in office might be destructive of democracy and stability. Hence, the Embassy and U.S. AID provided massive support to a so-called citizens' group, the *Red Ciudadaña* (Citizens' Network—many of the same opportunists who had earlier been involved in agrarian reform, family planning, sustainable development, etc.), to oppose Balaguer, find alternative candidates, and rally oppositionist sentiment. It brought in the National Endowment for Democracy (NED), the National Democratic Institute (NDI), and a host of well-paid civil society, political party, and elections experts to help support this campaign. Depending on one's politics, of course, one can approve or not approve of the Embassy's actions, but one should not confuse these embassy fronts and their political machinations with genuine indigenous, home-grown, or grassroots civil society, let alone with democracy. Moreover, once the Embassy had accomplished its short-term political goal, the funds for this ostensible "civil society" organization quickly dried up, leaving the Dominican groups high and dry and without sufficient support in most cases to survive. Many of their leaders then accepted high positions within the succeeding government (perhaps their goal all along in mobilizing civil society), thus leaving the fledgling civil society groups bereft of both funds and leadership. Such manipulation of "civil society" by governments and foreign embassies happens all the time, and we need thus to distinguish between genuine civil society of the homegrown kind and that sponsored by states and outside powers.[12]

(16) Is Civil Society Self-sustaining?

The above discussion touches on an important point: Is civil society sustainable after the foreign support and funds are gone? The answer is, no one knows and it is likely to be a mixed bag of outcomes. The issue is important and fraught with policy implications because, if civil society is not sustainable once the outside support dries up, the political system may well fragment, disintegrate, and collapse—precisely the outcome that the civil society initiatives were designed to prevent. But it is just as likely that another scenario will play out and that quite a number of countries may be left with the worst of all possible worlds: traditional civil society (tribes, caste associations, patronage networks) undermined and destroyed under the impact of both modernization and U.S. pressures, but a fledgling modern civil society—political parties, interest associations, opposition groups— floundering because of popular indifference and a withdrawal of critical foreign funding. Here we need to distinguish between countries: Mexico may be sufficiently well developed and institutionalized that its civil society can survive U.S. Embassy machinations and funding shortfalls, but in the less developed, less well-institutionalized Dominican Republic, in Sub-Saharan Africa, in the Philippines, Indonesia, and East Timor, and in the small countries of Central America, the decline or withdrawal of outside funding for civil society groups, in the absence of very much home-grown associability, may well lead to societal unraveling and political breakdown.

(17) "Civil Society" as a Reflection of the United States

It is striking how often, when we speak of civil society, we have in mind a society that looks just like we do. And that when foreign funds are involved, the types of "civil society" supported tend to look just like their sponsoring groups in the United States. Take the case of the National Endowment for Democracy. For partisan reasons and to get the bill through Congress, NED consists of four constituent groups: the Republican and Democratic Parties' international affairs branches, big labor (the AFL-CIO), and big business (as represented through the U.S. Chamber of Commerce). This structure is, of course, a reflection of internal U.S. political power and interest-group relations, but whether a similar or imitative structure is appropriate for all other societies, cultures, and political systems is unlikely.[13] Similarly with other, more narrowly focused groups: what the Population Council, the National Wildlife Fund, and others have as their agendas may be quite appropriate in the United States but I am not sure the exact parallels, even mirrors of these groups, need to be established abroad. Civil society, it seems to me, needs to be variable and appropriate for diverse societies and cultures; patterning civil society in other countries exclusively or nearly so on our own model and society may be inappropriate and self-defeating, and ultimately lead to failure.

(18) Central Versus Local Controls

As liberalization and democratization have expanded in recent decades, we have seen a gradual dismantling—at least at the formal, legal, or constitutional level—of the authoritarian, corporative, or regulatory controls by which states control civil society. Democracy in short means not just parties and elections but a freeing up of associational life in general. For in most countries one cannot just go out as in the United States and organize an interest group; instead, the interest group must seek recognition and "juridical personality" from the state, and there is a vast web of regulations and corporative controls that is used to co-opt, control, and limit such group activities.

But while in many countries these corporative controls are being repealed at the national level, they are being reenacted at the local level (where most civil society groups operate) as local authorities force civil society groups to register, show their membership lists and sources of financing, and gain recognition from local officialdom. Of course, the power to grant recognition to a group also implies the power *not* to grant it. So while corporatism is often in decline at national levels and democracy triumphant, at local levels corporatism is often reemerging. Democracy in its formal form may thus not be incompatible with a high degree of illiberalism at both national and local levels, but then is that truly democratic?

(19) Civil Society as Romantic Vision?

Are the focus and hopes that have come to be centered on civil society realistic? Or are they the product of unwarranted idealism and romance? Is civil society another one of those concepts that inflate expectations, provide short-term employment for thousands of consultants, and then fall to earth again? So far, the results of all civil society efforts have been disappointing: slightly over 10 percent organized in any fashion in all of Latin America, far less so in Africa, the Middle East, and Southeast Asia. Surely civil society has done little so far to enhance democracy or development in Africa or the Islamic countries, and East Asia appears both not to want *or need* much in the way of civil society. In Peru and Venezuela, under authoritarian-populist leadership, civil society has all but been destroyed; Cuba has no or minimal civil society to speak of apart from the state; and, particularly in the small, underdeveloped, weakly institutionalized countries of Africa and Central and South America, the Rousseauian model of direct identification between leader and masses, *sans* civil society, continues to be attractive. Is civil society, which seems to many to be an agency of hope, really a clutching at straws?

(20) Can Civil Society be Exported?

So far, there is *not a single case* of the West being able to export its model *en toto* to other lands and cultures. By this, I mean not just the

Western model of civil society but, more basically, the cultural and social norms that undergird it, derived from the Renaissance, the Reformation and particularly its economic and political ramifications, the Enlightenment and its rationalist way of thinking, the industrial revolution, and the revolution of democracy in its Lockean, Madisonian, Jeffersonian form. *Parts* of the model—usually easily imitated institutional arrangements such as elections or parliaments—may be exported, both because people want them and because we put pressure on and leverage them; but usually not the underlying values of democracy (tolerance, egalitarianism, mutual respect) nor the vast webs of associability that Tocqueville described. Those are peculiar, particular, a part of our unique history, culture, and tradition; they cannot be packed up and shipped over in a container carton to countries where the culture, society, and traditions are distinct. Of course, we can get thin and pale imitations of civil society and democracy ("democracy with adjectives"—"limited," "controlled," "organic," "delegative," "Rousseauian," "Islamic," "Confucian," "corporatist") but not often the real thing. That takes two or three generations, as in Russia, not two or three years; and other than in only superficial ways it remains doubtful if civil society is transplantable from one model country to another. The result in most of these countries is what has come to be called "formal democracy" (regular elections and the like) but not "liberal democracy."

TOWARD THE FUTURE

Having said all of these skeptical things about civil society, let me also say that I tend to be in favor of the concept and what it implies in a policy sense. For most (not all) countries, a web of intermediary associations between the citizen and the state serves both to limit state power and authoritarianism and to serve as a transmission belt by which citizens can make their interests known to government officials. To the degree civil society is present, it *tends* (not always) to be good for the state, for society, and for democracy.

Extrapolating from the list of twenty reasons to be skeptical about the concept analyzed above, three problems seem to be especially important. The first is the incredible variety of civil society forms, their diverse underlying philosophical, social, and cultural assumptions, the frequently mixed and "crazy-quilt" patchworks that exist, the distinct definitions, meanings, and priorities accorded civil society. The second, related, is the problem of ethnocentrism: our (particularly American) inability to comprehend and accept forms (Confucian, Islamist, clientelistic, statist, corporatist) of civil society and state-society relations, let alone democracy, other than our own. The third problem is politicization of the concept—by everyone and for private political or economic purposes: local elites in Third World countries, foundations, the AFL-CIO, the Chamber of Commerce, AID, NED, U.S. embassies abroad, successive U.S. governments. Once that happens, and the issue gets enmeshed in our and other domestic politics and our politicized foreign policy, it is probably hopelessly lost, and we should, therefore, expect the gaffes, shortsightedness, and frequent misfires that have, in fact, occurred in many countries.

The ethnocentrism, biases, failures of understanding and empathy, private agendas, and all the other problems identified here may be a cause for despair among those, of whom I count myself one, who favor the growth of civil society. Three points need to be made. First, the civil society agenda, like the democracy one, is now so deeply entrenched in the international lending agencies, the foundations, and U.S. and other aid and foreign policy programs that it is certain to continue despite our reservations about it. Second, *on balance,* the concept of civil society and what it stands for—democracy, pluralism, participation, a group life apart from the state—are still worth working for, despite the frequent miscues and insensitivities. Third, therefore, let us continue with the program of assisting civil society, meanwhile trying to fix the problems indicated but not jettisoning the entire program. For even in its stumbling, bumbling, ethnocentric way, U.S. aid over time has produced some change, development, and the socioeconomic basis for greater democratization and civil society.

Civil society cannot "save the world," as some of its advocates have suggested. One is tempted to say cynically that civil society may have already peaked, that it is already too late, that we should forget about the idea and just wait for the next cure-all panacea to come down the pike. But that is too negative and, in fact, ignores the political process and positive factors that I have argued need to be taken into account. That in turn implies acceptance or at least understanding on the part of civil society advocates and practitioners of the compromises, mixed forms, and the frequent use and misuse of civil society in the political process. Hence, let us support and aid civil society—it is still a good idea—but do so with our eyes wide open, realistically, and recognizing both the opportunities and the limits that championing civil society in other people's countries offers.

NOTES

1. The title of a recent conference on civil society.

2. Robert Putnam, *Bowling Alone: The Collapse and Revival of American Community* (New York: Simon and Schuster, 2000).

3. Thomas Carothers, *Aiding Democracy Abroad: The Learning Curve* (Washington, D.C.: The Carnegie Endowment for International Peace, 1999).

4. Howard J. Wiarda, *Corporatism and Comparative Politics: The Other Great "Ism"* (New York: M. E. Sharpe, 1996).

5. Carothers, *Aiding Democracy*; and Lester H. Salamon and Helmut K. Anheir, *The Third World's Third Sector in Comparative Perspective* (Baltimore: Johns Hopkins University, The Johns Hopkins Comparative Non-profit Sector Project, 1997).

6. A balanced assessment is Carothers, *Aiding Democracy*; also Marina Ottaway et al. (eds.), *Funding Virtue: Civil Society Aid and Democracy Promotion* (Washington, D.C.: Carnegie Endowment, 2000).

7. Putnam, *Bowling Alone*.

8. Samuel P. Huntington, *Political Order in Changing Societies* (New Haven: Yale University Press, 1968); Linn Hammergren, *Development and the Politics of Administrative Reform: Lessons from Latin America* (Boulder: Westview Press, 1983).

9. A. H. Somjee, *Parallels and Actuals of Political Development* (London: Macmillan, 1986); Howard J. Wiarda, *Ethnocentrism and Foreign Policy: Can We Understand the Third World?* (Washington, D.C.: American Enterprise Institute for Public Policy Research, 1985).

10. Carothers, *Aiding Democracy*; Salamon and Anheir, *The Third World's Third Sector*; Ronald Inglehart, *Culture Change in Advanced Industrial Society* (Princeton: Princeton University Press, 1990).

11. Neil Harvey (ed.), *Mexico: Dilemmas of Transition* (New York: St. Martin's, 1993); and Wayne Cornelius et al. (eds.), *Transforming State-Society Relations in Mexico* (San Diego: Center for U.S.-Mexican Studies, Univ. of California, San Diego, 1994).

12. Christopher Sabatini, "Whom Do International Donors Support in the Name of Civil Society?" Paper prepared for delivery at the 2000 meeting of the Latin American Studies Association, Miami, March 16–18, 2000.

13. Howard J. Wiarda, *The Democratic Revolution in Latin America: History, Politics, and U.S. Policy* (New York: The Twentieth Century Fund, Holmes and Meier, 1990).

SUGGESTED READINGS

Adler, Glenn, and J. Steinberg. *From Comrades to Citizens: The South African Civics Movement and the Transition to Democracy*. London: MacMillan, 2000.

Alfonso, Dilla, and Michael Kaufman. *Community Power and Grassroots Democracy: The Transformation of Social Life*. London: Zed Books, 1999.

Alvarez, Sonia, and Arturo Escobar. *The Making of Social Movements in Latin America: Identity, Strategy, and Democracy*. Boulder: Westview, 1992.

Alvarez, Sonia, Arturo Escobar, and Evelina Dagnino, eds. *Cultures of Politics. Politics of Cultures: Revisioning Latin American Social Movements*. Boulder: Westview, 1998.

Aristotle. *Politics*. New York: Oxford University Press, 1965.

Assies, Willem, Gemma van der Haar, and Andre Hoekema, eds. *The Challenge of Diversity: Indigenous Peoples and Reform of the State in Latin America*. Amsterdam: Thela Thesis, 1998.

Atal, Yogesh, and Else Oyen. *Poverty and Participation in Civil Society*. Paris: UNESCO, 1997.

Axtmann, Roland, ed. *Balancing Democracy*. London: Continuum Books, 2001.

Basu, Amrita, ed. *The Challenge of Local Feminisms: Women's Movements in Global Perspective*. Boulder: Westview, 1995.

Beiner, Ronald, ed. *Theorizing Citizenship*. Albany: State University of New York Press, 1995.

Bentley, Arthur. *The Process of Government: A Study of Social Pressures.* Evanston, Ill.: Principia, 1935.

Bianchi, Robert. *Unruly Corporatism: Associational Life in Twentieth Century Egypt.* New York: Oxford University Press, 1989.

Black, Antony. *Guilds and Civil Society in European Political Thought from the Twelfth Century to the Present.* Ithaca: Cornell University Press, 1984.

Bratton, Michael. "Beyond the State: Civil Society and Associational Life in Africa." *World Politics,* 41 (April 1989), 407–30.

Burbidge, John, ed. *Beyond Prince and Merchant: Citizen Participation and the Rise of Civil Society.* Institute for Cultural Affairs International. New York: Pact, 1997.

Cantori, Louis. "Civil Society, Liberalism and the Corporatist Alternative in the Middle East." *Middle East Studies Association Bulletin,* 31, 1 (1997).

Carothers, Thomas. *Aiding Democracy Abroad: The Learning Curve.* Washington, D.C.: Carnegie Endowment for International Peace, 1999.

Carroll, Thomas. *Intermediary NGOs: The Supporting Link in Grassroots Development.* West Hartford, Conn.: Kumarian, 1992.

Chazan, Naomi, et al. *Politics and Society in Contemporary Africa.* Boulder: Lynne Rienner, 1992.

Clark, John. *Democratizing Development: The Role of Voluntary Organizations.* London: Earthscan, 1991.

Cornelius, Wayne, et al., eds. *Transforming State-Society Relations in Mexico.* San Diego: Center for US-Mexican Studies, University of California, San Diego, 1994.

Cornwell, Richard. "The Collapse of the African State." In Jakkie Cilliers and Peggy Mason, eds. *Peace, Profit, or Plunder? The Privatization of Security in War-Torn African Societies.* Pretoria, South Africa: Institute for Security Studies, 1999.

DeBary, W. T. *Asian Values and Human Rights: A Confucian Communitarian Perspective.* Cambridge: Harvard University Press, 1998.

Dekker, Paul, and Eric Uslaner, eds. *Social Capital and Participation in Everyday Life.* London: Routledge, 2001.

Department of State. *Focus on the Issues: Civil Society in the Americas*. Washington, D.C.: U.S. DOS, 2000.

De Tocqueville, Alexis. *Democracy in America*. New York: Random House, 1990.

Domínguez, Jorge. *Social Movements in Latin America: The Experience of Peasants, Workers, Women, the Urban Poor, and the Middle Sectors*. New York: Garland, 1994.

Durkheim, Emile. "The Solidarity of Occupational Groups." In Talcott Parsons, ed. *Theories of Society*. New York: Free Press, 1965.

Du Toit, Pierre. *State-Building and Democracy in Southern Africa: Botswana, Zimbabwe, and South Africa*. Washington, D.C.: U.S. Institute of Peace, 1995.

Eckstein, Susan, ed. *Power and Popular Protest: Latin American Social Movements*. Berkeley: University of California Press, 2001.

Edwards, Michael, and David Hulne, eds. *Beyond the Magic Bullet: NGO Performance and Accountability in the Post Cold War World*. West Hartford, Conn.: Kumarian, 1996.

Ehrenberg, John. *Civil Society: The Critical History of an Idea*. New York: New York University Press, 1999.

Farrington, John, David Lewis, S. Saish, and Aurea Miclat-Teves, eds. *Non-Governmental Organizations and the State in Asia: Rethinking Roles in Sustainable Agricultural Development*. London: Routledge, 1993.

Fisher, Julie. *The Road from Rio: Sustainable Development and the Non-Governmental Movement in the Third World*. Westport, Conn.: Praeger, 1993.

Foweraker, Joseph. *Theorizing Social Movements*. Boulder: Pluto, 1995.

Fowler, Alan. *Civil Society, NGOs and Social Development: Changing the Rules of the Game*. Geneva: United Nations Research Institute for Social Development, 2000.

Fox, Jonathan. *The Politics of Food in Mexico: State Power and Social Mobilization*. Ithaca: Cornell University Press, 1992.

Fox, Jonathan, and L. David Brown, eds. *The Struggle for Accountability: The World Bank, NGOs, and Grassroots Movements*. Cambridge: MIT Press, 1998.

Fox, Jonathan, Ann Craig, and Wayne Cornelius, eds. *Transforming State-Society Relations in Mexico: The National Solidarity Strategy.* San Diego: Center for US-Mexican Studies, University of California, San Diego, 1994.

Fukuyama, Francis. *Trust: The Social Virtues and the Creation of Prosperity.* New York: Free Press, 1995.

Gellner, Ernest. *Conditions of Liberty: Civil Society and Its Rivals.* New York: Penguin, 1994.

Gierke, Otto. *Political Theories of the Middle Ages.* Cambridge: Harvard University Press, 1987.

Glaser, Daryl. "South Africa and the Limits of Civil Society." *Journal of Southern African Studies,* 23 (March 1997), 5–25.

Grugel, Jean, ed. *Democracy Without Borders: Transnationalisation and Conditionality in New Democracies.* London: Routledge, 1999.

Hall, John. *Civil Society: Theory, History, Comparison.* Cambridge: Polity, 1995.

Hann, Christopher, and Elizabeth Dunn, eds. *Civil Society: Challenging Western Models.* London: Routledge, 1996.

Harbeson, John, Donald Rothchild, and Naomi Chazan, eds. *Civil Society and the State in Africa.* Boulder: Lynne Rienner, 1992.

Harvey, Neil, ed. *Mexico: Dilemmas of Transition.* New York: St. Martin's, 1993.

He, Baogang. "The Idea of Civil Society in Mainland China and Taiwan." *Issues and Studies* (June 1995), 24–64.

Huntington, Samuel. *The Third Wave: Democratization in the Late Twentieth Century.* Norman: Oklahoma University Press, 1991.

Inglehart, Ronald. *Culture Change in Advanced Industrial Society.* Princeton: Princeton University Press, 1990.

James, Estelle. *The Nonprofit Sector in International Development.* New York: Oxford University Press, 1989.

James, Wilmot, and Daria Caliguire. "Renewing Civil Society." *Journal of Democracy,* 7 (January 1996), 56–66.

Janoski, Thomas. *Citizenship and Civil Society: A Framework of Rights and Obligations in Liberal, Traditional, and Social Democratic Regimes.* Cambridge: Cambridge University Press, 1998.

Jaquette, Jane, ed. *The Women's Movement in Latin America: Participation and Democracy.* Boulder: Westview, 1994.

Kamrava, Mehran, and Frank Mora. "Civil Society and Democratization in Comparative Perspective: Latin America and the Middle East." *Third World Quarterly,* 19, 5 (1998), 893–915.

Kim, Ksunhyuk. "Civil Society in South Korea: From Grand Democracy Movements to Petty Interest Groups." *Journal of Northeast Asian Studies* (Summer 1996), 81–97.

Korten, David. *Globalizing Civil Society: Reclaiming Our Right to Power.* New York: Seven Stories, 1998.

Kotze, Hennie, ed. *Consolidating Democracy: What Role for Civil Society in South Africa.* Stellenbosch, South Africa: University of Stellenbosch, 1996.

Kotze, Hennie, and Pierre Du Toit. "The State, Civil Society, and Democratic Transition in South Africa." *Journal of Conflict Resolution,* 39 (March 1995), 27–48.

Kuperus, Tracy. "Building Democracy: An Examination of Religious Associations in South Africa and Zimbabwe." *Journal of Modern African Studies,* 37, 4 (1999), 643–68.

Larana, Enrique, Hank Johnson, and Joseph Gusfield, eds. *New Social Movements: From Ideology to Identity.* Philadelphia: Temple University Press, 1994.

Lathan, Earl. *The Group Basis of Politics.* New York: Octagon Books, 1965.

Lehmbruck, Gerhard, and Philippe C. Schmitter, eds. *Patterns of Corporatist Policy-Making.* London: Sage, 1982.

Locke, John. *Two Treatises on Government.* New York: Cambridge University Press, 1960.

Lovatt, Debbie. "Islam, Secularism, and Civil Society." *The World Today* (August/September 1997), 226–28.

Lowi, Theodore. *The End of Liberalism: Ideology, Policy, and the Crisis of Public Authority.* New York: Norton, 1969.

MacDonald, Laura. *Supporting Civil Society: The Political Role of Non-Governmental Organizations in Central America.* New York: St. Martin's, 1997.

Madison, James. *The Federalist*. Washington, D.C.: Thompson & Homans, 1831.

Makoto, Iokibe. "Japan's Civil Society: An Historical Overview." In Yamamoto Tadashi, ed. *Deciding the Public Good: Governance and Civil Society in Japan*. Tokyo: Japan Center for International Exchange, 1999.

May-sing, Yang. "NGOs Promote a Civil Society." *Taipei Journal* (October 27, 2000), p. 7.

McAdam, Douglas, ed. *Comparative Perspectives on Social Movements*. New York: Cambridge University Press, 1996.

McGrann, James, and R. Kent Weaver, eds. *Think Tanks and Civil Societies: Catalysts for Ideas and Action*. New Brunswick, N.J.: Transaction, 2000.

Meyer, David, and Sidney Tarrow, eds. *The Social Movement Society: Contentious Politics for a New Century*. Lanham, Md.: Rowman and Littlefield, 1998.

Migdal, Joel. *Strong Societies and Weak States*. Princeton: Princeton University Press, 1986.

Mohanty, Manoranjan, Partha Nath Mukherji, and Olle Tornquist, eds. *People's Rights: Social Movements and the State in the Third World*. Thousand Oaks, Calif.: Sage, 1998.

Monshipouri, Mahmood. "Islamism, Civil Society, and the Democracy Conundrum." *The Muslim World*, 57 (January 1997), 54–66.

Moody, Peter. *Tradition and Modernization in China and Japan*. Belmont, Calif.: Wadsworth, 1995.

————. "East Asia: The Confucian Tradition and Modernization." In Howard J. Wiarda, ed. *Non-Western Theories of Development*. Fort Worth: Harcourt Brace, 1999.

Morales, Isidro, Guillermo de Los Reyes, and Paul Rich, eds. *Civil Society and Democratization*. Thousand Oaks, Calif.: Sage Periodicals, 1999.

Near East Center. *The Civil Society Debate in Middle Eastern Studies*. Contributions by James Gelvin, Augustus Norton, Roger Gwen, and Diane Singerman.

Olvera, Alberto. "Civil Society and Political Transition in Mexico." *Constellations*, 4, 1 (1997), 105–23.

Ottaway, Marina. *Africa's New Leaders: Democracy or State Reconstruction*. Washington, D.C.: Carnegie Endowment for International Peace, 1999.

Ottaway, Marina, et al., eds. *Funding Virtue: Civil Society Aid and Democracy Promotion*. Washington, D.C.: Carnegie Endowment for International Peace, 2000.

Posusney, Marsha Pripstein. *Labor and the State in Egypt*. New York: Columbia University Press, 1997.

Putnam, Robert. *Making Democracy Work: Civil Traditions in Modern Italy*. Princeton: Princeton University Press, 1993.

_____. *Bowling Alone: The Collapse and Revival of American Community*. New York: Simon and Schuster, 2000.

Pye, Lucian. *Asian Power and Politics: The Cultural Dimensions of Authority*. Cambridge: Harvard University Press, 1985.

_____. "Civility, Social Capital, and Civil Society: Three Powerful Concepts for Explaining Asia." *Journal of Interdisciplinary History*, 29 (Spring 1999), 763–82.

Reilly, Charles, ed. *New Paths to Democratic Development in Latin America: The Rise of NGO-Municipal Collaboration*. Boulder: Lynne Rienner, 1995.

Rosenberg, Robin, and Richard Feinberg, eds. *Civil Society and the Summit of the Americas*. Coral Gables, Fla.: North South Center, 1999.

Rosenblum, Nancy, and Robert Post, eds. *Civil Society and Government*. Princeton: Princeton University Press, 2002.

Rousseau, Jean Jacques. *On the Social Contract*. New York: St. Martin's, 1978.

Rubin, Jeffrey. *Decentering the Regime: Ethnicity, Radicalism, and Democracy in Juchitan, Mexico*. London: Duke University Press, 1997.

Sabatini, Christopher. "Whom Do International Donors Support in the Name of Civil Society?" Paper presented at the 2000 meeting of the Latin American Studies Association, Miami Fla., March 16–18, 2000.

Salamon, Lester. *The Civil Society Sector*. Baltimore: Johns Hopkins University Press, Comparative Nonprofit Sector Project.

_____. *The Rise of the Nonprofit Sector.* Baltimore: Johns Hopkins University Press, Comparative Nonprofit Sector Project.

_____. *Social Origins of Civil Society.* Baltimore: Johns Hopkins University Press, Comparative Nonprofit Sector Project.

Salamon, Lester, and Helmust Anheir. *The Emerging Nonprofit Sector: An Overview.* Manchester: Manchester University Press, 1986.

_____. *The Third World's Third Sector in Comparative Perspective.* Baltimore: Johns Hopkins University Press, Comparative Nonprofit Sector Project, 1997.

Schechter, Michael, ed. *The Revival of Civil Society: Global and Comparative Perspectives.* New York: St. Martin's, 1999.

Schmitter, Philippe, and Gerhard Lehmbruch, eds. *Trends Toward Corporatist Intermediation.* Beverly Hills, Calif.: Sage, 1979.

Seligman, Adam. *The Idea of Civil Society.* New York: Free Press, 1992.

Shin'icki, Yoshida. "Rethinking the Public Interest in Japan: Civil Society in the Making." In Yamamoto Tadashi, ed. *Deciding the Public Good: Governance and Civil Society in Japan.* Tokyo: Japan Center for International Exchange, 1999.

Slater, David. *New Social Movements and the State in Latin America.* Amsterdam: CEDLA Publication, FORIS, 1985.

Smith, Brian. "NGOs in International Development: Trends and Future Research Priorities." *Voluntas,* 4, 3, 301–25.

Splichal, Slavko, Andrew Calabrese, and Colin Sparks, eds. *Information Society and Civil Society: Contemporary Perspectives on the Changing World Order.* West Lafayette, Ind.: Purdue University Press, 1994.

Stephen, Lynn. *Women and Social Movements in Latin America: Power from Below.* Austin: University of Texas Press, 1997.

Stevens, Evelyn. *Protest and Response in Mexico.* Cambridge: MIT Press, 1974.

Syed, Anwar. "Democracy and Islam: Are They Compatible?" In Howard J. Wiarda, ed. *Comparative Democracy and Democratization.* Forth Worth: Harcourt Brace, 1999.

Tadashi, Yamamoto, ed. *Deciding the Public Good: Governance and Civil Society in Japan.* Tokyo: Japan Center for International Exchange, 1999.

Tarrow, Sidney. *Power in Movement: Social Movements and Contentious Politics.* New York: Cambridge University Press, 1998.

Truman, David. *The Governmental Process.* New York: Knopf, 1951.

Van Cott, Donna Lee, ed. *Indigenous Peoples and Democracy in Latin America.* New York: St. Martin's, 1994.

Veltmeyer, Henry, and Anthony O'Mally, eds. *Transcending Neoliberalism: Community-Based Development in Latin America.* Bloomfield, Conn.: Kumarian, 2001.

Warkentin, Craig. *Reshaping World Politics: NGO's, the Internet, and Civil Society.* New York: Rowman and Littlefield, 2001.

Warren, Kay Barbara. *Indigenous Movements and Their Critics: Pan-Maya Activism in Guatemala.* Princeton: Princeton University Press, 1998.

Weisbrod, Burton. *The Voluntary Nonprofit Sector.* Lexington, Mass.: Lexington Books, 1977.

Welch, Claude E., Jr., ed. *NGOs and Human Rights: Promise and Performance.* Philadelphia: University of Pennsylvania Press, 2001.

Wiarda, Howard J. *Corporatism and Comparative Politics.* New York: M. E. Sharpe, 1997a.

_____. *Cracks in the Consensus: Debating the Democracy Agenda in U.S. Foreign Policy.* Washington, D.C.: Center for Strategic and International Studies, 1997b.

_____. *The Democratic Revolution in Latin America.* New York: Twentieth Century Fund, Holmes and Meier, 1990.

_____. *The Soul of Latin America: The Cultural and Political Tradition.* New Haven: Yale University Press, 2001.

_____. "State-Society Relations in Latin America: Toward a Theory of the Contract State." In Howard J. Wiarda, ed. *American Foreign Policy Toward Latin America in the '80s and '90s.* New York: New York University Press, 1992.

Wiarda, Howard J., ed. *Comparative Democracy and Democratization.* Fort Worth: Harcourt Brace, 2001.

_____. *Non-Western Theories of Development*. Fort Worth: Harcourt Brace, 1999.

_____. *Politics and Social Change in Latin America*. Boulder: Westview, 1993.

Williams, Heather. *Social Movements and Economic Transition: Markets and Distributive Conflict in Mexico*. Cambridge: Cambridge University Press, 2001.

Williamson, Robert. *Latin American Societies in Transition*. Westport, Conn.: Praeger, 1997.

ABOUT THE AUTHOR

Howard J. Wiarda is professor of political science and comparative labor relations, and holder of the Leonard J. Horwitz Chair in Iberian and Latin American politics at the University of Massachusetts, Amherst. He is also senior associate of the Center for Strategic and International Studies (CSIS) and senior fellow at the Woodrow Wilson International Center for Scholars, both in Washington, D.C. His many books include *New Directions in American Politics, Third Edition, Introduction to Comparative Politics, European Politics in the Age of Globalization, Non-Western Theories of Development, Comparative Democracy and Democratization, Corporatism and Comparative Politics,* and *Latin American Politics and Development.*

INDEX